Dedication

This book is dedicated to my niece, Logan Elizabeth DeWitt. Here are to the times, Logan, when you may think no one else believes in you...we always will.

I really need to thank my family—Mom, Greg and Bari—for putting up with me during this project and especially for the encouragement (those pizza dinners helped, too). Then, there are my friends: Mary & Ed (it's the funny quotes that work!), Sheri & Michael, Bonny, Albert, Bryan, Deb & Rudi, Michelle & Isaac, and everyone else. It always helps to know you have friends; especially the one's that put up with you in times like this!

Thank you, also, to Chuck O. who started this project with me, and now Brian H. and Jim O. who are finishing it with me. It's been an interesting trip, hasn't it!

Competitive Intelligence Competitive Advantage

Michelle DeWitt

Abacus
www.abacuspub.com

Printed in the U.S.A.

ISBN 1-55755-324-6

10 9 8 7 6 5 4 3 2 1

Contents

Part 4:   161 - 196
The Case Studies

The Internet

Part 1

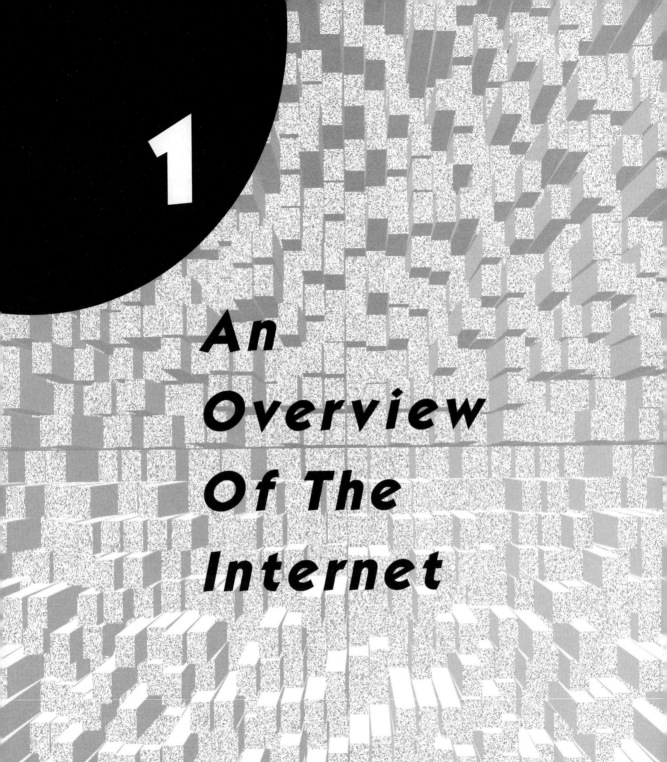

1

An Overview Of The Internet

An Overview
Of The Internet

A Little History

It may seem hard to believe, but the Internet will celebrate its 28th anniversary this Labor Day. In the 1960s the U.S. Department of Defense wanted to decentralize its computer network so that the loss of one network hub (due to hostile governments or natural catastrophe) wouldn't bring down the entire network, effectively severing lines of government and military communication. To this aim the Defense Advanced Research Projects Agency created and administered the ARPANet, the first incarnation of today's Internet.

The first Interface Message Processor, a predecessor to today's routers, was installed at the University of California, Los Angeles, (UCLA) near Labor Day, 1969. By the end of that year four defense research sites were connected to the ARPANet.

Between 1969 and 1983 there were many advances in the lower-level inter-networking protocols that led to the TCP (Transmission Control Protocol) and IP (Internet Protocol) used on the Internet today. In 1973 the first international connections were established, to England and Norway. The BBN (Bolt Beranek and Newman, Inc.) opened Telnet, a commercial version of ARPANet, in 1974. Although not officially documented, Queen Elizabeth reportedly sent her first e-mail in 1976.

In an effort to link over 100 computer scientists through electronic mail, THEORYNET was created at the University of Wisconsin in 1977. Two years later Tom Truscott and Steve Bellovin created USENET between Duke University and the University of North Carolina, establishing the groundwork for today's newsgroups.

CSNET (Computer Science NETwork) came about in 1981 to provide a dial-up capability for electronic mail, letting users without access to ARPANet dial into CSNET through modems and regular phone lines. Several universities feeling left out of ARPANet soon joined CSNET. In 1983 a gateway between CSNET and ARPANet was established so users of either could access the resources of both.

Because ARPANet was expanding so rapidly, it split into two different networks in 1983: ARPANet and MILNET. MILNET became integrated with the Defense Data Network, which had been created the previous year, to provide secure military data transmissions. The next year, 1984, saw the introduction of moderated USENET newsgroups.

In 1986 the National Science Foundation created NSFNet to link its supercomputing centers with universities. NSFNet assisted in the implementation of commercial networks which were opened to the public and allies of the United States. The combination of the NSFNet and the regional networks that resulted from it became known as the *Internet*.

In 1987 the NSF signed an agreement for MERIT (Michigan Educational Research Instructional Network) to manage the NSFNet backbone. MERIT—a nonprofit networking corporation of state universities operating out of Ann Arbor, MI—then entered into an agreement with IBM and MCI for computing technologies and communication facilities. The ARPANet—the very project that started it all—ceased to exist in 1990, replaced by NSFNet and MILNET.

The first relay between a commercial electronic mail carrier, MCI Mail, and the Internet was established in 1990 through the Corporation for the National Research Initiative (CNRI). About the same time CompuServe began offering similar services through Ohio State University.

In 1992 the World Wide Web was released by the European Laboratory for Particle Physics—more commonly known as CERN (the French acronym for Centre Europe'enne pour la Recherche Nucle'aire, which translates to Center for Nuclear Research, which later changed its name to reflect its current field of research).

The NSF created InterNIC in 1993 to provide specific Internet services, such as registering domains and providing information services. Both the United Nations and the White House went on-line in 1993, the latter with electronic mail addresses for President Clinton, Vice-President Gore and First Lady Hillary Rodham Clinton. At the same time, businesses and the media began taking a strong interest in this seemingly new medium called "The Internet."

Today, Tomorrow And Beyond

Open Market's Internet Index estimates that 9 million adult Americans use the World Wide Web daily. Approximately 85,600 domain names are registered each month. And if this is not enough, in the third quarter of 1996 advertising revenue on the Web generated 66 million dollars—a 43% increase over the second quarter. Now that is commerce!

We live in a world that is just not as big as we once thought. Simple e-mail programs allow us mere mortals to correspond with people all over the world in only minutes. Since most Internet Service Providers now offer unlimited access time for a flat fee, it seems as if it is free to "reach out and touch someone" on the 'Net. Sending a letter via snail mail (regular post) takes an average of 10 days just to get one way, plus the postage and actually mailing it. Now you can feasibly send a letter to someone halfway around the world and receive a response in minutes, without leaving your house or office.

You can shop for wool goods from a store based in Scotland; visit a virtual pub in Ireland; plan your next vacation, including booking flights, hotels and car rentals; find out how much the toys in your attic are worth; or even locate that goofy friend from college you had lost track of—all on the Internet, right from your computer. In an era when time seems to be our most precious commodity, being able to access these services at home and after hours seems to be the only sane option.

The Internet has enabled us to become armchair researchers—full of facts, but on what and how useful that information may be remains somewhat of a mystery. It's sort of like a huge garage sale, utilizing the theory that "one man's junk is another man's treasure."

Just consider the number of sites available to browse from the estimated 20 million domain names; if you have done any "surfing," you know that there is a lot of junk out there. But as more information becomes available, we get better at organizing it and finding what we want. Either with the skills to navigate the Internet on our own or with the help of something or someone else, we find more information than we ever thought possible.

On-line newspapers, magazines and commercial sites allow us the luxury of news and information that is world wide and instantaneous. Stock quotes and industry reports are as easy to review as comic strips. In an age when Competitive Intelligence is gaining prominence, the Internet is the one tool that allows companies and businesses of all sizes immediate access to important information.

2

Getting Connected To The Internet

Getting Connected To The Internet

Getting connected to the Internet is not quite as mystical or difficult as some would believe. Basically, with a computer (Mac or PC), a modem, communications software and a telephone line you are ready to connect to the Internet and start your intelligence gathering! Very quickly, here is a crib-note on selecting and setting up your access to the 'Net:

A computer

Just to begin, you need to decide between a Macintosh or an IBM compatible. You most likely already have one or the other at home or work; if you're buying another, get the same kind to ensure compatibility.

The old rule of thumb was that if the main use was for word processing or accounting-type functions, an IBM compatible was your method of madness. If you were looking at a computer more for graphic capabilities, a Mac was your weapon of choice. But now there are so many software packages available for both platforms that it is much more of a personal preference.

Warning: Most users are diehard believers in one or the other—but not both. I highly recommended that you personally test both systems before you make the decision, for both have very good attributes. Should you consider the IBM compatible, your processor should be at least a 486 model.

While mega-stores such as Best Buy and Office Depot are able to offer low prices due to their volume buying, you need to remember that they may not offer much technical support, especially after the purchase.

Buying from a smaller, local dealer greatly increases your chances of getting satisfactory technical support. Yes, most computer manufacturers offer technical support for their systems, but I am sure that you have heard the stories of being on hold for over 45 minutes just to be told that the support team cannot answer your question, or that there is now a fee for the information required to solve that particular problem, and the list goes on.

Don't forget to review the technical specifications of the computer, such as memory capacity, how big is the hard drive, etc. Magazines such as *Home PC*, *PC Computing*, *Mac User* and many others frequently review different brands and models and offer shopping tips for new computer buyers.

A modem

If your computer does not have a modem, you will need one. The modem translates your computer's digital language into analog information for transport across ordinary phone lines, and renders incoming analog data into digital terms for your computer.

A modem's speed is usually expressed in kilobits per second (Kbps), and indicates how quickly it can move information (bits). The 28.8Kbps is the slowest modem I can recommend. 57.6Kbp is the fastest standard modem available, but most Internet services are not up to this speed yet.

Hayes is the best known manufacturer of modems, and most other brand modems are labeled "Hayes-Compatible." U.S. Robotics is the next most popular. You will find little price difference between similar models of modems, as the market is so competitive.

If there is any chance that you will know your Internet Service Provider or on-line service *before* you purchase the modem, ask your service what modem they use so you can maximize your connection.

Please keep in mind (for both the computer and the modem) that technology changes at the snap of your fingers, so get as fast a system as you can afford! Trust me on this advice; I have upgraded a few computer systems in my time and it NEVER ceases to amaze me how fast the technology changes—not even one year ago the 14.4Kbps modem was the standard!

Printer

While this is not a necessity, you'll appreciate having the ability to print what you will find on the Internet. Like most of the components, prices have become much more reasonable for printers lately, even color printers.

When selecting a printer, remember that print quality is rated by dots per inch (dpi). A higher dpi will result in a much better printed piece. Your printer options (in order of cost) are: dot-matrix, ink-jet and laser. A dot-matrix printer usually will not have the quality (dpi) you will want and they are generally very noisy. In their favor, they tend to be quite inexpensive in both upfront cost and in maintenance, such as replacing ribbons.

An ink-jet printer enables you to get a higher print quality while being fairly fast. Due to the technology and competition, prices for these are very reasonable and the color option does not tend to affect the price much. Do beware of the cost for replacement ink cartridges, as some have separate cartridges for each color, while others only have two—one for the black and another for color printing.

Laser printers are the fastest and produce the best quality results. However, they are also the most expensive. Also, they depend on individual color sticks for each of the four primary colors. Depending on for what else you will be using the printer, ink-jet printers seem to be the most popular, offering good quality at an affordable price.

You may also want to consider a many-in-one device. These are geared primarily to small office/home office users and bundle such services as printing, scanning, copying, faxing, telephony and more into one machine. These can reduce desk clutter and offer needed services. As they continue to become less expensive, expect to see more of these in homes before too long.

Most stores have printers set up so that you can run a test print to evaluate speed, print quality, noise and other factors. As printing in color often slows the printer down, you should run both a color and monochrome test to see just how that affects the speed. You may be surprised at the difference in color and print quality from one manufacturer to the next.

Internet Service Provider/On-line Service

You also need to establish how you will connect to the Internet. There are two ways to do this: Internet Service Providers (ISPs) and on-line services. An ISP—such as Voyager, IBM, On Ramp and Sprint—will generally get you e-mail and a direct connection to the Internet. This is the truest sense of the Internet as once you have a browser, the Internet universe is yours for the exploring!

An on-line service—such as America OnLine (AOL), CompuServe and Genie—provides you with more of an on-line community, where you can access e-mail, enter chat rooms with other members of your service provider or even go shopping.

The chat rooms allow you to converse with other members along the theme of the room you choose to enter (many different theme rooms are available, including Star Trek, Singles, Technology, Sports, etc.). As the conversation scrolls you type your comments and send it to the chat, where it is entered into the flow of conversation.

Remember that the shopping areas that seem quite cool are paying to be there, and most of the "stores" only offer a small amount of merchandise which can become quite mundane after a few visits. On-line services usually offer a search engine to access information on the Internet, but they do not necessarily promote use of the 'Net.

A big plus for these services, however, is that they are quite easy to sign on with. Almost everyone has received at least one disk from AOL for those "10 free hours of on-line time!" While they may seem bothersome to a lot of the recipients, just remember that AOL has an extremely large client base and many loyal users—because of the chat rooms and other services that are wrapped into an easy-to-use package. Ease of getting connected is a big plus for these larger Internet services. But remember, easy is not always better, especially in the long run.

One suggestion for finding which service is best for you is to get the latest issue of a publication like *Internet World* for reviews on various Internet Service Providers (ISPs) and on-line services. Another method is to consult the local UGs (Users Groups) or MUGs (Mac User Groups). These groups can usually be found by asking around among computer users.

Mac users often complain that these services are not very Mac-savvy, so all of you Mac users beware! If you already have access to the Internet at work or at school, you can use search engines (we'll explain these in a minute) to access information on services.

You'll find at www.yahoo.com/Business_and_Economy/Companies/ Internet_Services/Access_Providers/ a section listing ISPs nationwide. However, the best source may be friends or co-workers who are already connected. Just ask around, people are usually more than happy to tell you about their service.

Do not rule out local providers (try the Yellow Pages) as they often offer extremely cost-effective packages in order to compete with the larger, national companies. Before you sign up you should clarify a few things with the services: What type of backup systems do they have and how many access lines are available? It is essential that the provider has either a local telephone number or a toll-free number for accessing their server. Otherwise you will be paying long distance fees just to connect, and that is where you will incur unexpected costs.

Dialer connection

We've explained the computer, modem, printer and Internet Service Providers. That only leaves the telephone line, and I do hope that you have that figured out by this point! While some alternatives are being researched for connecting to the Internet, the telephone cable is the best option for most businesses and almost all personal connections. T1 and T3 lines—which are much quicker—are also much more expensive and aren't a viable option for most people at this time.

Please keep in mind that after doing all of the above, there is a chance that your connection will not work due to errors within your computer files. It may be impossible to get onto the Internet until those are settled. Common problems occur within your DOS files for PCs or in your Systems Folder for Macs. This is the stage where purchasing your computer at the local dealer makes a lot of sense for that technical support! Or, hope that the Acme Company has a remedy for the solution (the Acme Company from the Road Runner cartoons always seemed to have a gadget for anything!).

3

Traveling Around The Internet

Traveling Around The Internet

An Introduction To Browsers

The World Wide Web is a system developed to provide hypertext access to documents via the Internet, wherever they are located. Browser software (simply called "browsers"), such as Netscape's Navigator and Microsoft's Internet Explorer, enables the user to browse documents posted on the WWW.

Hypermedia documents—which may include still and moving pictures and audio as well as text—can be accessed through the browser simply by clicking the mouse/cursor on an underlined or bold word or phrase. Note that only the *http://* and *gopher://* protocols are supported by browsers (Web protocols will be discussed momentarily).

Most ISPs make a browser available with their services. You can also download a particular browser from the company's site (www.netscape.com or www.microsoft.com in this case). Most sites you'll be using for your CI research (or for any browsing, for that matter) are configured for the latest version of these browsers, so it is wise to keep upgrading to maximize your viewing experience.

Plug-ins are applications that add to your browser's basic functions. Some of the more popular plug-in applications include: *RealAudio* (from Progressive Networks), which allows you to receive real-time radio broadcasts over the Internet; *Java* (from Sun Microsystems) and *Shockwave* (from Macromedia), which enable you to use enhanced multimedia functions; and *VDO-Live* (from VDONet), which allows you to view real-time videos over the Internet. Sites that have used plug-ins in their interface almost always have links to the sites of those applications in case you do not already have them.

Off-line browsers will be reviewed in Part Three as part of the research process. Using criteria you specify, these browsers automatically download and store sites and files from the Internet to create its own cache on your hard disk. While on-line or off-line, you can access the information from the stored files.

What About Those URLs?

Uniform Resource Locators (URLs) are now the standard methodology for locating information on the Internet. Also known as "Internet Addresses," URLs provide a lot of information about a particular site. Following are some examples for the Library of Congress:

```
http://www.lcweb.loc.gov/homepage/lchp.html
gopher://marvel.loc.gov:70
telnet://database.carl.org
```

The first identifier of an URL is the type of application used for a site, called the *Protocol*. The four basic types are:

http://	HyperText Transfer Protocol (the Web)		telnet	Method of using a remote terminal
gopher:	Text-based information server		ftp://	File Transfer Protocol

The second identifier of an URL is the host's site name. Using the above URLs, the hosts would be: lcweb.loc.gov, marvel.loc.gov and database.carl.org. Within this host name is the Domain type you will be visiting. Here is the traditional listing of those:

.com	Site for commercial purposes		.mil	U.S. military
.edu	Educational institution		.net	Network operation
.gov	U. S. government source		.org	Non-profit organization

Many nations have their own domains as well, such as *.ca* (Canada), *.au* (Australia) and *.sp* (Spain).

However, the Internet Ad Hoc Committee (IAHC) has also proposed seven additional "generic" top-level domains, which may be in effect soon:

.arts	Arts- and culture-oriented entities		.rec	Recreation/entertainment sources
.firm	Businesses		.store	Merchants
.info	Information services		.web	Sites focusing on Web activities
.nom	Individuals			

Understanding the components of an URL will assist you when you are looking at lists of matches on search engines, etc. Keep in mind that the *.com* sites are for commercial purposes and therefore are usually supported by paid advertising, etc. You can bet that there will be a noticeable difference in information contained on a *.com* site as opposed to a *.gov* site.

The final part of the URL is where the resource is located on that host. This describes the "path" of the information such as: "homepage/Ichp/html" and "70." This is similar to a computer's directory structure. In the first example, "html" would be a webpage in the "Ichp" directory, which is itself stored in the "homepages" directory.

Start Your (Search) Engines!

Search engines are the gateways to resources on the WWW. These applications are actually indices of WWW sites, searchable by topics or key words. Alta Vista, Lycos, Excite and Yahoo are a few of the more well-known search engines recognized by users. Depending on the information you are looking for, some of these search better than others. In Part 3 there will be a much more comprehensive discussion on a variety of search engines and their applications in collecting Competitive Intelligence.

Other Applications

There are many sites on the WWW that have applications available for users to download, often for free. Some of these software applications allow you access to both telnet:// and ftp:// files. Some sites specifically for this include www.shareware.com, www.software.com and www.softwareshop.com.

Depending on your industry, there may be several different software applications at your disposal. By just using "Applications" for your keyword with a search engine you will find plenty of these sites according to your interests. The medical industry/profession has a quite a few of these different software applications available. Even software not specific to your industry can be accessed.

4

A Few Tips Regarding Privacy On The Internet

A Few Tips Regarding Privacy On The Internet

There has been a lot of talk regarding privacy on the Internet. Both your personal and your business records of many kinds are easily accessible by anyone who has access to the Internet. If it seems eerie that so much information about you is available to any person for their perusal, consider this: most of the information that is available about you on-line is no more public than it was before; it is just that now more people can access it faster and easier. It used to be that only wealthy people or large companies could and would pursue the information, such as court documents and government filings. But the Internet has democratized this information for anyone with 'Net access.

However, there are a few things that you may want to keep in mind regarding other sources of information about you (other than public documents and filings). Were you aware that your e-mail messages can be read by someone else? Although the reports of e-mail having been intercepted appears to be quite small, you should consider e-mails to be electronic postcards rather than letters in sealed envelopes. Invincible Mail by Invincible Data Systems (www.incrypt.com) and PGPmail from Pretty Good Privacy (www.pgm.com) are two programs that can help safeguard your privacy. To date, both of these only offer their programs in a Windows format.

Also, did you know that just by visiting a site, you can provide that webmaster with information on what type of computer you have, what browser you are using, how long you looked at each part of the site and even what link you used to exit the site?

Just by using some basic Web tools, these webmasters are securing the information they need for reports on people like you who visit their site. Habits of site visitors (how much time was spent looking at particular files or what link was used to exit the site) are usually monitored for marketing reasons. When visitors return to the site, that information is again logged in so that patterns and profiles can be determined.

There is a site called the Anonymizer (www.anonymizer.com) that will act as a go-between for your computer and the sites you wish to visit, and it's free! By using this, you are assured that your identity is not revealed and it does not allow any cookies to be left. Until an upgrade arrives at the Anonymizer site, however, it is only running for the first half hour of each hour. They also have Terms of Service that you need to review before actually using it. These six conditions and restrictions that they need to impose on you guarantee it's continued existence.

To obtain even more information about you, webmasters use a software tool called "magic cookies." A cookie is a small piece of information (a crumb) that the site downloads to your computer's hard drive when you initially visit and reads each time you return—all without your knowledge. These are supposed to be helpful tools, such as storing a password to a site so that you don't have to re-enter it every time you visit that site. But they are also used to track information on perhaps an article that you reviewed or a product that you purchased from a site.

That information may then be sold to companies who want to know your habits. Fortunately, only the site where the cookie originated from can collect it and view it. Better yet, a cookie cannot obtain information from elsewhere on your hard drive, such as your e-mail address or your password for log-in. Now, if you would prefer to be warned about these little rascals, it is possible to have your browser alert you whenever a site attempts to set a cookie on your hard drive.

If you have Internet Explorer 2.0 and later, you should select **Options** in the **View** menu. There you should click the Advanced tab and then check the box that says "Warn before accepting cookies." With Netscape Navigator 1.0 and later, you need to get to the **Options** menu and select **Network Preferences**. Then click on the Protocols tab and check the box that says "Show an alert before accepting a cookie."

This way, you are given a choice of accepting or rejecting each cookie that a site wants to place. Some programs such as ZDNet's CookieMaster (www.hotfiles.com) and PGPcookie.cutter, from Pretty Good Privacy (www.pgp.com), allow you to delete existing cookies and intercept new ones. A big plus of some of these programs is the ability to set expiration dates for those cookies that you have allowed to be set. When warnings come up, they notify you of the file name and also when the cookie expires; the furthest cookie expiration date so far is 2039! Some of these programs also tally the number of cookies that have been attempted to be set on your PC.

Finally, another area of the Internet that can compromise your privacy is Usenet newsgroups. Newsgroups are forums covering almost any subject imaginable, where people can gather on-line and discuss matters esoteric and mundane with others around the world. But did you know that any message you post to a newsgroup can be traced by anyone through Deja News (www.dejanews.com)?

All postings to Usenet groups since 1995 are now on a searchable database. Deja News hopes to add their archived files from their start-up in 1979 to that database. If someone would see a comment you had posted to a particular group, that could reveal a little about your views and/or interests. However, if that someone collected everything you had posted in newsgroups, they would probably have a very good idea of what you were like.

If you would rather not have those old records available, you can e-mail Deja News to ask that they delete your old postings from the database. For future use and postings to newsgroups, you should type in "x-no-archive:yes" as the first line of your posting and Deja News will not archive that message.

Internet privacy issues and the possibility of federal regulations has gotten a lot of press lately. At this point we can only guess what form those regulations may take. But by educating yourself and others about privacy issues and techniques, individuals can become more responsible for their own information and how it is accessed. This could be the most important step in keeping federal regulations to a minimum and helping maintain the Internet's primary function: providing information on anything to everyone in the world.

Competitive Intelligence

Part 2

5

What Is It And Why Do I Need It?

What Is It And Why Do I Need It?

Competitive Intelligence has been around in one form or another since the very first business owner opened his/her operation—perhaps a fruit vendor in Adam and Eve's neighborhood (but that's a different story altogether!)—and was followed by a second. Of course, the first business owner wanted to know what the new place was selling and who was buying it.

This is the origin of Competitive Intelligence. Through time it's evolved into a much more complex practice, mostly due to the ever-increasing sources of information. A good business strategy is always founded in the information about your rivals that you need to stay competitive. Without it, the contest wouldn't seem fair.

The very mention of Competitive Intelligence gets people thinking of the CIA, Interpol, spies and often times, danger. While that is an exciting view of it, the truth is that Competitive Intelligence is a lot of research and analyzing of information, something many people would classify as, well...boring. However, successful application of CI can be very exciting, especially when your business thrives.

To be competitive in business today, enterprises of all sizes need to be aware of the importance of Competitive Intelligence. Surprisingly, only about 10 - 15% of companies report that they actively practice Competitive Intelligence. But how successful could a sports team be if it ignored CI?

A business isn't much different: a team of players actively competing against at least one other team. The team captain and other key players make it their responsibility to have all of the information about the opposing teams that they can get. In understanding the opponent's strengths and weaknesses and knowing how the opposition will react to certain situations, these key people are able to formulate strategies for each player to capitalize on the other team's known practices.

Why shouldn't this same practice be followed in business? With a business team consisting of all its workers, why wouldn't the president and key personnel try to gather all the information necessary to formulate plans for the company's competition, and ultimate survival? In a time when more and more companies are seeing the advantage of Competitive Intelligence, you will also see some companies caught with no game plan while the others develop research-based strategies and act on those plans.

In this era of quicker manufacturing turnaround, it is entirely possible for a company to lose a race that they never really entered because they didn't have important information on a competitor's new or revised products.

Experts agree that Competitive Intelligence is both an on-going study (or process) and an end product. The on-going study involves selecting, gathering, interpreting and distributing publicly held information that has strategic importance. This includes knowledge of products, competitors, a market or even an industry. It is not necessarily the trade secret of your competitor that you need, but rather the tactical and strategic intelligence that you can develop from the information sources available to you.

This is a *continuous* process, not an isolated study. Evaluating information accumulated through time makes it easier to predict behavior and responses. Then, by consistently monitoring and analyzing your competitors and the industry, you will be able to pick up on the fluctuations that you may not have seen during a "spot check."

It is important to realize that you will **not** catch everything, but the practice of CI will certainly lessen the impact of the oversight. The end product of CI is realized when you use some or perhaps all of your information for a specific action. This may include finding the pricing scheme for a new product from your competitor, what R & D projects are being pursued by your competitors (or which ones aren't), or possibly even confirming a rumor that your competitor is pursing a new industry with an existing product.

Quite simply, Competitive Intelligence acts as a filter for you, spotting new opportunities and helping you avert disasters. This is what happened between AT&T and MCI. When MCI was formulating a long distance service, their information gathering revealed that AT&T had no central database for its customers and so could not track when or how often its customers called each other. As MCI was just developing its database, they built in a process for tracking those customers. They used this advantage to offer a 20% discount to MCI customers who frequently called each other—the plan was, of course, Friends and Family. This campaign produced 5 million additional customers for MCI over 5 years, many of those taken from AT&T.

An example of using CI to avert a disaster involves Monsanto Inc.'s Nutrasweet unit. In 1991, customers told Nutrasweet sales reps that the US Food & Drug Administration was ready to approve Sucralose, a rival sweetener from Johnson & Johnson. The top managers at Nutrasweet proposed a 3 year, defensive ad blitz costing several million dollars just to defend its two-thirds share of the then $1.5 billion market.

However, the CI unit at Nutrasweet concluded—from various, carefully cultivated contacts and sources—that FDA approval was not imminent and that the ad blitz would be a waste of money. The Chairman and Chief Executive sided with the CI analysts and delayed the advertising. Five years later the FDA still had not approved Sucralose.

Competitive Intelligence does not assure success. There are, of course, cases of misinformation and of rival's countermeasures. An example of this is the case of a company that had invested in new technology that was difficult for the competitor company to track. Then the company announced the launch of their brand, only to delay it for a year. The competitor wasted an entire year's advertising budget in anticipation of defending their market share from the attack that didn't come. Plus, the original company was able to see how their competitor was planning on defending itself once the product was actually launched.

In a similar event, Ford paid up to $750 million more for Jaguar than they had expected. The speculation is that General Motors concluded that Ford was willing to pay almost any price to acquire the company, so they entered the bidding just to raise the final price.

A well-known example of countermeasures involves Kodak and Xerox. As the story goes, back in 1995 a Kodak copier sales person told a Xerox technician that he was being trained to service Xerox products. The Xerox technician told his supervisor, who relayed the report to the CI department. Using the information they could find—including Kodak's newspaper classified ad for people with Xerox product experience— Xerox confirmed the initial report that Kodak was indeed planning to service it's copiers.

However, because of the advance warning, Xerox introduced a Total Satisfaction Guarantee program, which allowed any Xerox Copier to be returned for any reason as long as official Xerox technicians had done all of the service work. By the time Kodak kicked off their new plan, Xerox had been selling its program for three months. Kodak offered to honor Xerox's guarantee, but their servicing gains weren't enough to offset the decreasing profits from copier sales. A few months later, Kodak agreed to sell almost all of it's copier business to Danka Business Systems PLC.

When hunting for Competitive Intelligence, let's remember a very simple rule: *Any* transaction that a company makes is a clue to it's overall strategy. This could be where they buy their office supplies (selected for cost and convenience) to the people they hire (chosen for field experience and knowledge of potential new markets) to where they buy their raw materials (cost vs. quality) to their pricing (based on overhead expenses and r & d costs).

Any of these transactions that you can uncover and piece together will give you a better understanding of their strategy and how you can formulate a planned response. Keeping in mind that the size of your company/business should not matter, consider the case of two health food stores, located within 10 miles of each other (only in different towns).

One owner was taking some boxes out after receiving an order when she found her competitor rummaging through her discarded boxes. He was in her dumpster, in daylight, checking to see where the orders had come from and what brands she was stocking. Another case involves an employee at a Kellogg cereal plant who, as he was pulling into the parking lot, saw a lot of unusual activity at the General Foods' Post plant across the street.

Upon further inspection, he found that they were delivering a German-made twin-screw extruding machine onto the loading dock, not the French-made model usually used in US cereal plants. He immediately went to a nearby store where he purchased a cheap camera and film. He then stood across the street from the Post plant and took pictures to document the machinery.

He concluded that perhaps Post had learned something about the German-made apparatus which Kellogg should know, since everyone was having troubles with the French-built machines. Noticing him, Post employees weren't thrilled, and even asked him to stop photographing, but the gentleman from Kellogg was standing on the far side of a public street, and they were unloading the machinery in plain sight. This fellow gained important business information just by keeping his eyes open. CI isn't all boring text research.

Keep the following questions in mind when planning your Competitive Intelligence:

1 Why do you need the information?

2 What information do you need for this?

3 What action do you expect to result from the information?

If you can keep the focus narrow and defined, you will find it easier to sleuth out the information for which you are looking.

Let's take a closer look at these questions. Let's assume that you are thinking of opening a hardware store. This will be a case where you begin your intelligence gathering in a broader manner than you normally would.

First, you should know about the industry in general. Collect information on the industry, such as its history and, more importantly, forecasting studies. You should also know your potential customers, both individuals and contractors. You will need information on the demographics of this industry, and then identify those demographics for your particular location. This information will lay the groundwork for the resources you should check regularly for the continuing process of Competitive Intelligence.

A more specific approach is needed when you want to know the pricing strategies of your competitors and what the market will bear. Here you would want to make a list of the essential information needed (such as competitors pricing, their after-sales policies and terms, their strategies for increased sales and so on). Once you have all of this information, you should be able to set your own pricing as a reflection of your competitors, your knowledge of the industry and your target customers.

Depending on your industry/business, the information you are seeking may vary quite a bit. Take an independent movie producer; when asked what he would like to know about the competition, he replied that it wasn't the competition he was concerned about. In his line of work having timely access to new book reviews was crucial for his job. By getting a hold on the books (and subsequently the authors), he may be able to option the book for a movie, thus giving him a leg up on the other movie producers who are looking for the same sort of story lines. For his case you would want sources of timely book reviews, such as the New York or the LA Times.

As more newspapers go on-line, you could check out some news sources for such information. Another possibility are periodicals and directories that cater to authors. There are sites on the Internet that target this group, too. Not only would you be able to scout for new talent at such places, but you could also contact the authors directly—either by e-mail or telephone—with an offer or to establish contacts for future use and reference. Periodicals and sites catering to the Independent film crowd can be good sources of ideas for upcoming films and can help one gauge reactions to films already in distribution.

When a small tool and die manufacturer was asked what information he would be interested in regarding his competitors, his response was that he was most interested in how the competitors were marketing themselves and what information they were using to do so. Since his manufacturing process was so specific, he felt he pretty much knew his competitors' manufacturing processes, just not how they were selling it.

So, for this case, you would want to find out how the competitors are marketing their manufacturing process. For this you'll find information regarding their advertising, industry listings (such as Thomas Register, etc.) and possibly even some industry reports.

Trade shows are an excellent source of how companies are marketing their products, too. It may even be possible to get some information out of your sales force. As they probably call on many of the same people that your competitor does, you will want to involve them in your quest for knowledge.

Some of this information could come from the Internet, too. As there are many sites that cover manufacturing, you may start by searching those sites for listings of the competitors. In doing so you will obviously find where they have chosen to be listed, and maybe better yet, where they have *not*. Also, what kind of information are they allowing to be posted? This could be an important clue to strengths and weaknesses in the competition. While most industry-specific sites have databases from which to search, they usually find items by company name and product name; how and what they list here could be significant.

By gathering all of this information, you may find that your competitors are focusing on price and timely delivery. Maybe now would be a good time to introduce a strong commitment to quality and service programs!

A fast food franchise owner was asked what sort of information he felt he needed to compete among the many different food chains, and he said that food quality and service were the major factors to consider. Depending on the type of food offered, he said price was not necessarily the main issue. By knowing the quality/constancy of both the food products and the service received from the competitors, he had what he felt was a good knowledge base on the local competitors.

By compiling a list of not only prices for certain food products, but also the consistency of service and quality, you may find all that you need for this project. However, in looking into different franchise policies and incentive programs, you may find information that can be of use, too. As many franchises are using the Internet to sell their units, you may well be surprised at how much information you can get from here. Another idea to consider is asking your customers. Depending where else his customers eat out, the concern of this owner may really be privately owned restaurants of similar fare instead of other fast food operators.

According to a commercial photographer's studio manager, what other photographers were charging or even specializing in was not the most important competitive information. Technology is her Competitive Intelligence focus. She felt that keeping up on the latest technologies, such as digital cameras and improved traditional equipment, was the first step to remain in the running.

Next, knowing what agencies handle which key accounts was crucial. If one agency lost Company A's account, who got it? Looking long term, she felt that niche markets—and who handled the accounts in those markets—were the key to longevity. So for her we want to get information on the current technologies in the industry, and maybe along the way find some agency information.

You can target industry and technical publications and editors that will probably get you headed in the right direction. Trade shows are a great way to actually see what some of the new technologies are, and if it is something you want to pursue now or perhaps wait until the next upgrade is ready.

However, it may be also be a good idea to check out the competition, as they may have made a technological advance that you did not know about, and should. Also, if these competitors have an Internet site, you may be able to find out which agencies are their clients. Of course, you can always contact the client and/or the agency directly, too.

It should be re-emphasized that all of the information you will be gathering is part of public record. An article in the October 11, 1996, issue of *Business Week*, reports that "Corporate Intelligence becomes illegal espionage when it involves the theft of proprietary materials or trade secrets." It is *not* advisable to get into any situation while seeking information that would be construed as illegal or immoral.

If you have questions about what you or someone working for you are doing, simply ask yourself if you would want to be "caught" doing it; if you answer No, then you darn well better *not* do it! And this past October President Clinton signed legislation that makes industrial espionage a federal crime, punishable by up to 15 years in jail and $10 million in fines. That's another good reason to stay on the sunny side of the street.

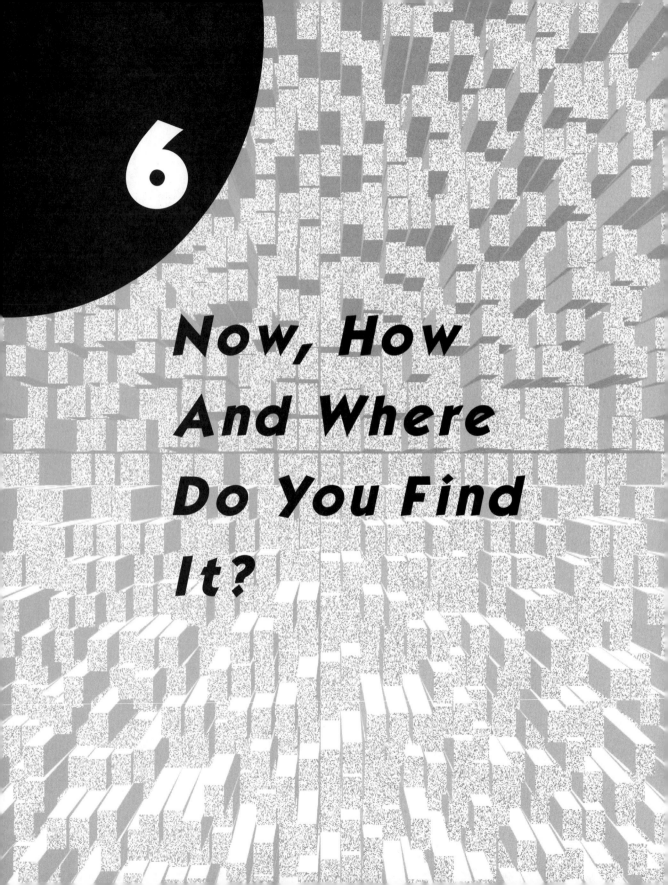

6

Now, How
And Where
Do You Find
It?

Now, How And Where Do You Find It?

Put On Your Sleuthing Hat—You're Ready!

In general, experts believe that 80 - 90% of the information needed for any given CI project is available through publicly-accessible channels. Keeping in mind that this information is not always in plain site, it is still part of public record somewhere. Here are some sources to plumb for information:

- Your and your competitor's employees, customers and vendors

- Key contacts: analysts, academics and scientists

- Government filings (such as SEC documents)

- Trade publications and their editors

- Local area publications

- Trade shows

⬤ Miscellaneous public documents (such as speeches)

⬤ Court transcripts

⬤ The Internet

Before you begin your sleuthing, it should be clear once again that honesty and integrity are important. If you are going to do the research, you should be prepared to give your name and company where necessary (and appropriate). As the resources we have already mentioned are publicly available, your competitors may not be overjoyed at your ambition, but they can hardly blame you. If they are not already doing this themselves, they should be!

As Competitive Intelligence Chief for Ryder System, Inc., Faye Brill believes that 80% of what you need to know about your competitors is right inside your company. That's a lot of information, and many companies have set up formal channels to filter information from employees to the top levels of the company for review.

Because your sales force is out in the industry, they are well placed to glean tidbits of information on competitors that customers may innocently tell them, perhaps regarding a new product or confirming information you have already heard. Your personnel department can get you a list of employees who have been formerly employed by your competitors. Provided that they are not bound by nondisclosure agreements, they can provide valuable insights into your competitors' systems (or operations). This could include sales reporting, accounting, even database management.

Knowing how your competitors use and organize their information can be significant. If they have good systems, you can learn from them and improve your own; or if they are not so good, then you can capitalize on their limitations (remember the AT&T vs. MCI case).

Vendors can also be a hot bed of information; once engaged in simple conversation about the local economy or industry, you may well be amazed at what these people know about hirings, downsizing and even new product developments.

It is vital to have contacts in position to relay relevant information to you in a timely fashion. Some experts even suggest putting well-connected individuals on a retainer to give you nonproprietary information as they learn it. Some also suggest having these people sign nondisclosure agreements to build a networking plan.

Industry analysts and academics are key contacts for trends and developments in any industry. These people usually have great contacts in many areas including the government and private sectors, as much of what is forecast depends on information from those same sources. One place to look for analysts are trade associations. Information on these associations can generally be found in trade publications, or try Yahoo!'s Professional Organizations list at www.yahoo.com/Economy/ Organizations/Professional.

If your competitor is using the local university resources to assist in product development—and if it is a publicly funded school—project and progress reports may be available for those projects. Also, the university may have a special interest in your competitor (due to departmental foci), and may have case studies or special projects involving them. You can find contact information for universities at the public library and there are several sources on the Internet (using search engines, etc.). It may be best to start with the head of the departments where you think the projects may have originated.

Scientists are important for information regarding new government regulations or new materials for industries, such as processing, pharmaceutical, etc. While there may not appear to be anything going on, they may have information on an old process about to be revised or even of some things that never made it through to the end; something that you may want to try again or completely stay away from.

The National Institute of Standards and Technology is responsible for research by experts and top executives in such industries as automated manufacturing, biotechnology and computer sciences. This office can be reached (301) 975-3058 or at their website (www.nist.gov).

Government documents such as SEC, OSHA, Ownership and even patent filings can be very useful and are public knowledge once filed. All of the reports and requests that you yourself need to file for your business must be filed by everyone else, too. All you have to do is request that information from the government agencies.

You may want to target the city and state of each competitor and request the guidelines to required corporate filings, since each state varies. By contacting the tax assessor in a targeted area you can find building descriptions that include the size of each building as well as the property values. One company reported that researching a Uniform Commercial Code filing (which reports what the company has financed) revealed a detailed listing of all assets in the plant. This UCC report, along with incorporation records and limited partnerships are available through the Secretary of State's office.

As with many of these government agencies, you may want to start in the Federal Government section of your telephone book for locations and contact information. You can also try the U.S. Business Advisor on the Internet (www.business.gov) or contact them at: National Technical Information Service, Technology Administration, U.S. Department of Commerce, Springfield, VA 22161. This website was specifically designed to assist businesses in accessing the information, services and transactions of the federal government.

Trade publications and their editors may be obvious, but are so useful they deserve mention. Reports of new plants, acquisitions, mergers, downsizing and personnel changes can be important footnotes in your research. These editors are privy to industry information almost immediately. Since editors must be very careful what they print, they also take great care in authenticating any piece of news they come upon, making their information very reliable.

Don't overlook the reporting and interviewing of key personnel in the industry. You may be quite surprised at what the President of your competitor reports in such situations. In case you need to find publications for your industry, try business libraries. They should have publications on hand such as the SRDS (Standard Rate & Data Service) or other publications that list periodicals by industry. These will list not only the publication titles, but also the editors' names and contact addresses—especially useful if the editor has a separate office.

Much like trade publications, local publications for your competitor's area offer many bits of information such as job postings, layoffs, etc. Reviewing the job postings can get you a good idea of what position(s) they are looking for and the wages they are offering.

Most importantly, what type of qualifications are they looking for; perhaps knowledge of a related industry in which they had previously not been involved? One software company was tipped off to what may not have been considered a rival when the other company—traditionally hardware only—ran an ad for persons with experience in specific software applications. Another case involved a company in a small town that laid off more than 250 people within one year. That news never made the trade publications, but it sure made the local paper.

What your competitor may not want as industry news, they may not be able to keep out of the local publications. One local business journal each week lists the Federal and State Tax Liens, along with Bankruptcy notices and District Court cases. Listings of these local and regional business publications can usually be found in the appropriate telephone books at the public library.

Trade shows can also be an arena of information. Most companies have their brochures available for anyone walking by to take with them (including you, as you also walk by). That new piece of equipment that the competitor has been bragging about—it may be on display and operating to show the potential customers how wonderful it is. It is amazing what is left on display after convention hours—from brochures to actual products—with no one at the booth to discourage you from reviewing.

Trade shows are also a great way to check out the competitors' personnel, as many executives are there along with the sales, marketing and sometimes even the research & development groups. The many industry functions during these shows are good chances to socialize with those from the "other camp," although here we stress again that you do not misrepresent yourself (sometimes quite difficult anyway, if your name badge reports your company along with your name!).

Public speeches are also good sources of CI. Many speeches are made at industry events such as trade shows. However, you may surprised what the president of your competitor says at the company's annual 4th of July celebration, Dedication of the new City Sewage Plant or even the St. Patrick's Day Celebration/Parade. If you do not have a plant or sales office nearby, a competitor may not think twice about revealing sensitive information. These speeches are usually available at the local library.

Transcripts of court cases are an interesting arena. As long as the information is pertinent to a case, the courts do not care how sensitive is the information being revealed. You can ask your company's legal council or contact a legal librarian regarding legal databases and indices.

One company found sales and profit figures for a privately held company it monitored in the transcript of an Environmental Protection Agency hearing. The targeted company was trying to prove that it could not pay a large EPA fine, and in the process sent its CFO to testify at the hearing. As he submitted financial records for the previous three years to show the company's financial status, those reports became part of the hearing, and therefore became a matter of public record by being included in the minutes of the hearing.

A Directory of Electronic Public Access Services to Automated Information in the United States Federal Courts is available at www.uscourts.gov/pubAccess.html via the Internet or you can write them at: The Electronic Public Access Program Manager, Office of Court Programs, AO, Washington DC 20544. The site (and office) has contact information for the U.S. Supreme Court, U.S. Circuit Courts of Appeal, U.S. District Courts and the U.S. Bankruptcy Courts.

Last, but hardly least, is the Internet. With oodles and oodles of information accessible by most anyone, CI has finally been brought to the front lines for strategic business planning. A lot of the resources already mentioned can also be accessed on the Internet. For those that you cannot access directly, you will probably find the telephone number or address to contact them. Never before has so much information been available to so many people. Keep in mind that by cutting the time and usually the costs involved in retrieving the necessary information, the Internet makes it much more possible for not only you, but also your competitors, to practice timely Competitive Intelligence.

Kick Back And Let Someone Else Drive

As this book is designed to help you glean the information you need for good CI practices, it should be mentioned that there are, of course, professional individuals and companies that you can hire for CI. You may not have the financial resources to support a full time, internal CI department, and this venue allows you to pursue the information you need even if you and the company are not able to.

Also, if you want to get market information such as benchmark reports, it is quite wise to have a third party conduct the research so that you do not have to misrepresent yourself during the process. Depending on where your competitors are located—locally, regionally, nationally or even globally—you may even want to hire more than one firm.

By using the already mentioned resources, and a few that you may not have authority to access, these people can help you right out of the starting block. They will assist you in defining what your goals are for the project and how to accomplish them. You may want to contract with them just for the basic outline and some guidelines on where to look (besides the resources listed above) or you may want long term assistance.

Who you decide to hire may depend your and your competitor's locations, the industry, your budget, among other factors. Keeping in mind that these people do this for a living, this may be the best path to take if time is a major factor. Let there be no mistaking this: CI is very time consuming, especially when you are just starting out. If your first big CI project involves news of a new product introduction by one of your competitors and you just heard of it, this is a time to *seriously* consider hiring someone outside the company who is familiar with your industry and has necessary contacts already in place.

Founded in 1986, the Society of Competitive Intelligence Professionals (www.scip.org) consists of CI professionals from companies and consulting firms all over the world. SCIP helps individuals to further understand and practice Competitive Intelligence through educational and networking opportunities.

With programs such as an annual conference and regional chapter meetings, and a quarterly publication, the Society reports on new techniques for effective CI and the latest trends in technology. They understand and encourage their members to learn from each other as much as trying to find new methods.

Currently, SCIP has 4945 members representing 44 countries. SCIP is headquartered out of Alexandria, Virginia, but they also have European Question Centers in Brussels, Belgium, and London, England. The annual fee to join is quite reasonable, especially when considering the benefits of networking with so many different people involved in Competitive Intelligence.

7

Great! Tons Of Data, But What Do You Do With It?

Great! Tons Of Data, But What Do You Do With It?

Well, you have defined your goal and begun collecting the information necessary to accomplish it. Data is cheap and easy to find, thanks in part to the Internet and the many databases available on-line. But it is the summation of your findings, the Competitive Intelligence, that is valuable. In comparing this to a jigsaw puzzle, the little pieces of information that you have just don't seem to make a lot of sense individually. However, once you start categorizing them and getting the framework together according to your goal, you will find that you have a pretty good picture in the end.

While it may seem childish, it may help to physically organize your data so you can better mentally organize it. Remember those term papers in high school and college, the ones where you were supposed to arrange your ideas on note cards? Well, those habits and methods can help you again. As you will be collecting a lot of data, and hopefully on an ongoing basis, those note cards may be a pretty good idea after all.

If you start out collecting general data on the industry and your competitors, you could have categories (or headings) such as *Industry Information*, plus maybe *Competitor A, Competitor B* and *Competitor C*; and actually make piles (or files) for each category. This way you can record the pertinent information on each note card, along with the source and date of each to organize your findings.

Great! Tons Of Data, But What Do You Do With It?

Chapter 7

If you are looking into specific issues such as pricing and financial information on competitors, you could have subheadings for *Pricing, Policies* and *Financial*, for examples. Then you'll know where to find specific information when you want it.

There is a good chance that you collected too much information; maybe some that you really do not need or maybe even the same information from different sources. You may even find that you don't have enough, and that you'll have to keep looking; but by now you have a good idea of what the missing pieces are. As mentioned earlier, the practice of Competitive Intelligence is a lot of research and analyzing!

Many companies are making their CI reports available throughout the company via intranets or even newsletters. When employees are using the information that they help gather, everyone is involved in the dissemination of the results. An important note, though, is that if your company is disclosing the information to all (or even most) of its employees, you should have some policies in place to safeguard against that information leaving the company.

You should be extra careful if you are using e-mail to distribute the reports, as it is very easy to "forward" (or pass along) the messages outside the company. Be sure to identify the information as confidential!

One of the most common reasons that CI fails is that the directors do not support or even believe in it. Executives in businesses need to recognize the potential of the Internet and how it pertains to their particular situations. This is true of executives at all sizes of companies, from the mega-corporations to small start-ups.

However, if the top executive level does not support this practice—by both understanding it and allocating funds and personnel—it becomes impossible to pursue it to the degree that it would help in the strategic planning for the company.

Great! Tons Of Data, But What Do You Do With It?

Chapter 7

It may be necessary for managers to make a clear presentation to the executive level that points out both the specific benefits and the anticipated investments required for a strategic CI plan. This presentation should include how the competition has been using the Net, how others have effectively used it and how your company will benefit from using it.

The Internet & Competitive Intelligence

Intelligence

Part 3

8

One Plus Two Equals Three

One Plus Two
Equals Three

While many larger companies are limiting the time allowed on-line to employees, or banning it altogether, the smaller enterprising companies are maximizing its potential. They're proving the Internet is a vast frontier of information that includes the Competitive Intelligence they need to maintain and move ahead in today's markets. Now, more than ever, technology is playing a major role in the way we review, conduct and forecast business. It not only affects us immediately, it also affects us globally.

Because its timeliness, not only are newspapers available on-line, but many newsletters are being published on the Internet before they go to print. Along with this is the diversity of news groups and the sheer volume of Internet sites by companies in every industry all over the world that contribute to the "Information Overload" on the Internet. While it's true there is much "useless" information posted on the Net, this book will attest to the legitimate and useful sites and information in the name of Competitive Intelligence!

Now, before we fully step onto the soap box to further tout the virtues of the Internet for CI purposes, let's clarify what the intentions are for this book. The Internet is not to replace other methods of research and obtaining information.

As with any new method or tool the Internet is to be used as another means of tracking the information you need. This may include finding addresses or telephone numbers of experts or editors in your industry if they are not accessible by e-mail or through news groups. It may include getting the address of the government offices in the city or state of one of your competitors to request copies of filings, if not accessible by e-mail. You may find reference to an article for which you can contact a business library. In these cases, the Internet facilitates the process of obtaining the information.

Rules when sleuthing

Finally, there are few rules to keep in mind when sleuthing on the Internet. While we have covered some of this before, it bears repeating as the rules may be just a bit different for the Internet.

Abide by any legal restrictions

If you're doing research for your company, or even company related, make sure you understand all legal restrictions. Then make sure you follow them. Depending on your industry and position within the company, you may need top-level clearance to send e-mail to suppliers or even potential clients.

Monitor your e-mail

Always remember that your e-mail leaves a trail. Regardless of any programs that you may buy, this is simply another way to communicate and many of the same rules for other means of communication apply. Never offer bribes and never exchange price information with your competitors.

Also, be careful of messages that you pass along to others, especially if you had an agreement with the original sender to keep it confidential. Be very careful not to use names or companies associated with the names concerning your research as seemingly innocent comments may be construed as damaging by someone else.

Don't misrepresent yourself

It may be acceptable to browse a competitor's site from an Internet service provider or a site (such as Anonymizer) that can protect your identity. However, you most certainly should identity yourself by name and company when posting to newsgroups, sending e-mail (including if you have the audacity to send an e-mail to your competitor while at their site), and of course, subscribing to mailing lists.

If you're collecting information for a report, state that very clearly so that there is no mistake. Also, make sure you use the information for how you were planning to use it.

Misinformation: do you or don't you?

The answer here is "NO!!" As you should be aware by now, you leave tracks everywhere you go on the Internet. Any information that you intentionally release to throw off the competition will probably be traced back to you. Once you have cried wolf, your credibility will be gone before you can type in the apologies.

Don't ever try to hack into a competitor's intranet

No matter how ingenious the means may be, it's simply not acceptable. PUBLIC information is the key to Competitive Intelligence and essential for its continued growth.

Resources Specific To The Internet

One of the biggest advantages to the Internet is the direct access to experts all over the world in about any country. We often just consider the Internet as a place from which to retrieve information. We tend to forget that we can contact most of those people who wrote the magazine article or research paper we found so helpful.

Establishing an e-mail network is quite easy. It affords everyone the luxury of responding at their convenience instead of a telephone call that could catch someone at a bad time. You shouldn't be shy about contacting those writers and researchers for additional information. Articles are usually cut short not for lack of content but because of space limitations . Also, keep track of the individuals that you meet during business; most will have e-mail addresses on their cards. If not? Ask if they have one and write it on the card.

Also monitor discussion groups (listserv) and newsgroups (Usenet). A listserv combines e-mail and a listserv server to broadcast a message to many people. Once you have broadcast your message, it is delivered to everyone in your mailing list's own e-mail. They can then broadcast to the entire group in response or just reply directly back to you.

By subscribing to an industry mailing list, you'll stay informed on what's happening in your industry as well as keeping an eye on your competitors. Better yet, it also keeps you abreast of news regarding your clients and potential clients. By subscribing and contributing to the list, you can add to your collection of experts from around the world.

Usenet also allows cyber citizens to interact with each other. This is, however, similar to a bulletin board where there are many messages posted for your review. An example of a search engine that searches newsgroups is called Deja News found at www.dejanews.com. By using keywords to search for, say, discussions on your competitors and their products, you can also monitor what is being discussed about your company.

One person noted that even though there can be a lot of speculation going on, the "rumor mill" often is closer to the truth than you might have imagined. That posting you read may tip you off to a new product change or launch or may even clue you in to a press release or industry event that you had missed. You can also post your response or question.

There is the case of a researcher at a chemical company that needed the number of packages of cake mix shipped in a recent year. She posted her inquiry on BUSLIB-L (the business librarians' discussion group) and had an answer that day from another corporate information specialist. He was able to provide her with the value of cake mix retail sales for the year she needed, plus he passed on the reference source publication.

In another example, a man had questions about left-handed cooking gadgets. Using newsgroups, he used the keywords "cooking", "gourmet", and "left" to try to narrow down his options. He finally settled on a food & cooking newsgroup and posted a message asking people what left-handed cooking utensils they would be interested in, what they currently use, and where do they buy them. In less than 50 minutes he had responses that included a woman who had owned a left-handed specialty shop telling him what items sold and what items she still had boxes of; one person who was looking for a left-handed can opener; and another who wanted left-handed oven mitts. Two of the responses also listed specialty shops across the country for left-handed merchandise.

As you can see, using these services can help you with market needs and responses to new products and even existing products.

The Internet has created one of the most unusual and, sometimes, the most promising source for competitor information: your competitor themselves. With more companies having Internet sites, the chances are quite good that your competitors are already residing in the cyber community. Unless they require passwords for access to the their sites, there is little the competitor can do to keep you from peeking at their site. One company reported that within 48 hours of starting their web site, all their major competitors had visited at least once.

As many companies tend to put more information than may be necessary on their sites, these regular visits could yield interesting results. Take, for instance, what one company's CI department found while scanning a competitor's site. They came upon a preview of a promotion to be announced at an upcoming trade show. The company that found the preview reworked their exhibit and pricing strategy in time for the show and lessened the impact of the competitor's announcement.

There was another case of a company that asked their CI professional to look into another company they were considering buying. One of the key points to the deal was the other company's position in the European market. This company felt that the other was overstating their information and weren't offering much else. This gentleman, upon visiting the targeted company's Internet site, found a copy of the CEO's speech to a British Industry group that discussed in some detail their market penetration and share in vital European markets. Comparing the speech content with the information that they already had, they were able to get a much more solid picture of the market share. Due to this Net work, they were able to negotiate a lower, final price on the deal.

As with most sources for information, you must be very careful with the information that you collect. The information contained on the Internet should be reliable. Unfortunately, you cannot be completely assured that will happen. Although most anyone can have a web page – and you will see some very well designed web pages by individuals – there is no guarantee the information contained on those are accurate. If you come across a piece of information that just seems too good to be true...verify it before you act on it! Keep in mind, there's a lot of misinformation and disinformation out there, especially with CI efforts on the rise.

Survival Guide

As it has been said before, CI is not easy nor fast. This is especially true in the beginning. Remember the Boy Scout motto: Be prepared! Well scouts, here are a few things to remember for your survival in the world of Competitive Intelligence gathering.

Organize

First, be sure that your area is clear of everything you do not need. Keep some scratch paper and a pen available for miscellaneous notes. Next, be sure that you have good lighting. Check to minimize the glare from the screen and from overhead lights. Last, be sure that you have comfortable seating. You will be amazed how quick the time goes by, so you better be ready.

Using your bookmark option

Yes, most browser software comes with a "bookmark" option. Usually all it requires is that when you get to a web site or specific web page, you can click the "bookmark" icon and it will store that URL in a collection. As you may not have used this option before, check it out before you continue. Often, your browser will have pre-loaded your bookmark file with several web sites already. You can keep them, but if you have the patience and a few minutes, sort through them now to avoid confusion later.

Stay focused

By this time, you should know what information you need for your CI project, be it specific to a product, competitor(s), or the industry. While using the various resources already described and more that will follow, you must stay focused!

It's very tempting to visit other sites or categories while you're researching your project. If you happen to wander off, either write down the URL, bookmark it or print it (the URL should print at the top of the page). Pay attention so you don't become lost!

Patience

Being patient is sometimes the hardest part. There will be times when every URL you enter is incorrect or when the links you start following end up in some obscure cyber mall. There are other times when you just seem to have the golden touch and you get all the information you were looking for; go buy a lottery ticket! Remember that lots of information is not the goal; good, hard data is what you need for your strategic planning. If you look for it, it will come.

Once you have established your sources, it's a good idea to run frequent information audits. That is simply reviewing the types of sites you're monitoring on a regular basis to be sure that they're still appropriate and make sure that your bookmarks reflect only the relevant sites.

9

Batter Up!

Batter Up!

Beware: the following is not for the weak at heart. Serious research and analytical skills are at work here!

Search Engines

We're starting with search engines for one simple reason. Unless you know the URL for specific sites or sites with good links, there isn't a way to get the information for which you're looking.

Types of search engines

Before continuing, we need to mention the slight differences in the types of search engines. One is the catalog-type search engine, such as Yahoo and Magellan. They act as registries, or listings, based on a description usually submitted by the Webmaster of a particular web site.

The other is an actual search engine-type that is based on a summary of the contents of millions of Web sites. Some of these search the entire text of a web page and others search only the text in the headers and page titles.

Search engines use automated software agents (usually called *spiders*) that visit each Web site within the public areas of the Web. Spiders record each address for a detailed record of what is available and where it's available.

Let's review a few things to keep in mind when using a search engine so you don't become lost before you begin. The first thing you may want to do is to read the Tips (or Help) section at each search engine's site you use. Since not every search engine searches the same way, you need to know how to best phrase your searches right from the beginning.

Also, you'll want to be as specific as possible. For example, you need to specify that you're looking for tool & die companies that are located only in Alabama. Otherwise, you'll end up with tool & die companies all over the world. If you're getting thousands of documents back in response, don't panic immediately. Most search engines list the returns in descending order so the best matches will appear first. Your best matches will usually be in the top ten and seldom beyond the top twenty.

You can always go back and refine your search, too. By using such methods as Boolean terms ("AND", "NOT" or "OR") you may be able to polish your search up a bit. Again, a lot of this can be found in the Tips section of the search engine but more realistically, it's trial and error.

CI and search engines

Regarding the subject matter, CI, the following are some brief outlines on search engines that were found to be the most useful for business information.

The basic criteria we used for a "good" search engine includes:

Write-ups for each "hit."

Whether the URLs are listed for each "hit."

If the "hits" are relevant to the search subject entered. For our purposes, a "hit" is any response that you get from a search.

Examples of search engines

The following sites are listed in alphabetic order (not necessarily order of preference).

Alta Vista
www.altavista.digital.com

Digital Corporation's AltaVista allows you to use a full-text search when searching the Web or Usenet groups. They claim their index gives you access to over 31million pages found on 627,000 servers – with 1,158,000 host names – and over 14,000 Usenet news group articles.

You also have your choice of search methods:

Simple

The Simple query works with + (for a required word or phrase), - (for a prohibited word or phrase), "" (to keep words and phrases together in an order) and * (to include suffixes such as "-ed", "-ing", etc.).

Advanced

The Advanced query works with Boolean terms that include AND, OR, NEAR and NOT. This option also has a two tiered search with Selection Criteria that act as a search field and Results Ranking Criteria that sort on a ranking field. This option also allows you to use a date filter range to help narrow your search.

Live Topics has been recently introduced to this site for another effort to help you in your searches. Enter your keyword(s) as usual and submit it for search. Then a Live Topics option appears at the top of the results page. If you choose it, another page is displayed with related keywords in a format setup for "checking" the ones you want to include and those that you want to discard. It's very similar to a Boolean technique and you may find it easier to use.

Excite
www.excite.com

One of the criteria for a "good" search engine was the display of URLs for returns, but it's not offered by Excite. However, this did prove to be useful for business related information so that was overlooked.

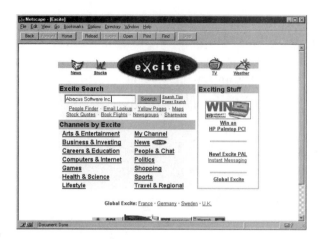

Excite offers two search options:

Basic
The Basic search uses Intelligent Concept Extraction (ICE) logic. Its searches are based on questions or phrases posed in everyday language (i.e., no boolean terms are needed). It will group words and phrases to look for several matches.

Advanced
The Advanced search uses not only the Boolean terms AND, AND NOT and OR but also + (for required words and phrases) and - (for prohibited words and phrases).

You can also choose to search the following:

➢ The Web Selected Sites (sorting by topics that include Science/ Engineering, Business/Companies/Manufacturing, etc.)

➢ Current News (includes Related Articles) and Newsgroup Postings (through Deja News)

➢ City.Net Travel Guide

Both searches offer a More Like This option for each result posted. In their own words "More Like This gives you a list of documents similar to a document you really like." An example of this was if you selected More Like This at an association return, it would then list similar returns that provided the same type of information, such as other associations, etc.

To search by subjects, Excite also offers Channels by Excite that include:

- ➤ Arts & Entertainment
- ➤ Business & Investing
- ➤ Carrers & Education
- ➤ Computers & Internet
- ➤ Games
- ➤ Health & Science
- ➤ Lifestyle
- ➤ My Channel *(we'll review this a little later)*
- ➤ News
- ➤ People & Chat
- ➤ Politics
- ➤ Shopping
- ➤ Sports
- ➤ Travel & Regional

HotBot
www.hotbot.com

HotBot claims to search over 54 million documents and over 4 million "recent" Usenet articles using a full-text search. Instead of worrying about the Boolean terms, etc., HotBot has options that mimic those terms in an easy to use format.

You can search the Web or Usenet News by All the Words, Any of the Words, The Exact Phrase, The Person, Links to this URL and The Boolean Expression. Furthermore, you can specify how many results to return and either Full Descriptions, Brief Descriptions or URLs Only.

To get even more specific, you can use Modify, Date, Location, and Media Type. Modify allows you to choose between Must, Should or Must Not contain The Words, Exact Phrase, The Person, or Links to this URL. Date allows you to specify Whenever, Within the last (X) (Months), After or Before or even On (Month) (date), 19(XX).

Location is unique in that it offers Any Place, Cyber Place (hotwired.com, .edu) and Geo Place (Africa, Europe, North America, etc.). Media Type allows you to choose from Image, Audio, Video, Extensions, Shockwave, VRML, Javascript, VBScript, Java, Active S and more.

Before you shrug this one off, try just the basic search using the simple options and you may be surprised at how easy it is and how accurate.

Infoseek
www.infoseek.com

"Proof of Intelligent Life on the Net" is their claim. Your search can be a specific question, a phrase in quotations or even an uppercase name.

You can chose to search:

➤ The Web

➤ Usenet News Groups

> News Wire

> Industry & Local News

> E-Mail Addresses

> Web FAQs

> Premier News
(consisting of 7 major news organizations such as CNN, NY Times, and Washington Post)

> Company Profiles
(includes detailed information on over 45,000 leading public & private companies)

You can use common capitals, commas, double quotes, a plus sign and a pipe "|". The pipe requests a search within a search. For example, if you entered "Automobiles|Fords", the search is narrowed to documents with automobiles mentioned and then only those with Ford mentioned.

Infoseek also offers the Ultraseek option. It features:

> Automatic Name Recognition

> Phrase Searching

> Plain English Queries

> Find All Word Variants

> Case Sensitive Searching

> Field Based Searches

Now, to get even more specific, the Ultraseek option offers "special searches" that include Imageseek (by way of Interpix), Site Search, Link Search, URL Search and Title Search.

If that's not enough for you, Infoseek also has what they claim to be the biggest Web Directory for you to explore. You can explore by the following topics:

- ➤ Arts & Entertainment
- ➤ Business [News]
- ➤ Computers [News]
- ➤ Education
- ➤ Finance & Investment
- ➤ Getting it Done
- ➤ Health
- ➤ Internet [News]
- ➤ Kids & Family Fun
- ➤ Politics [News]
- ➤ Shopping
- ➤ Sports
- ➤ Travel & Leisure

Lycos
www.lycos.com

Your basic search at Lycos can search The Web, Sounds, Pictures, Top 5% Sites or even UPS Tracking numbers.

It uses a few unique search options. They include:

Exact match

Use a period "." after the word you want to search for if you want an exact match. It will search only for web sites that contain that word.

Partial match

If you only know part of a name or word, use a dollar sign ($) after the partial name or word. For example, if you're looking for Mississippi, try miss$ in the search.

Excluding words

You can also use a hyphen (-) to exclude certain words from your search.

The Lycos Custom Search includes the options of Matching Any Term (OR) All Terms (AND) or 2 Terms through 7 Terms. You can also chose a Loose, Fair, Good, Close, or even Strong Match. For your display options, you can display 10, 20, 30 or 40 results per page along with Standard, Summary or detailed Results.

This is another site that offers WebGuides. You can chose from 18 categories, such as News, Travel, Science, Business, Technology, Government and Money. An editorial team regularly updates these categories to include news headlines, features, mini-directories and predefined Power Searches for your searching convenience.

Open Text Index
www.index.opentext.net

As with all the search engines reviewed (and those that were not), you need to be aware of a few unique features when searching for those tidbits of information on the Internet.

You have the option of Searching for This Phrase or These Words for the Simple Search. Since the Simple Search doesn't search for plurals, you'll need to submit "tool" and "tools" separately. Also, if you're looking for acronyms, try both the short and long versions, such as VW and Volkswagon.

Finally, you'll need to check both the American and British spellings, such as "color" and "colour."

You can use AND, OR, BUT NOT, NEAR and FOLLOWED BY in addition to Boolean strings. Once your results are returned, you do have a Refine Your Search option that refines your existing search by combining it with a new search (basically the Power Search method). The Power Search allows you to search within Anywhere, Summary, Title, First Heading or URL using linking terms or AND, OR, BUT NOT, NEAR and FOLLOWED BY.

Ways to decrease your searching time

Some searches can require a long time to complete. So, if you want to reduce your searching time, or perhaps try a different approach when searching, the following sites offer search engine capabilities for more than one search engine. Keep in mind that most search engines, like those we've talked about above, search in an unique way. Therefore, this can be at times a tricky and more time consuming way of searching.

The following all offer multiple searching from one query:

Dog Pile
www.dogpile.com

This site offers 23 search engines, over 6 Usenet and 3 FTP databases by which to search. You can request that it search 1 (The Web, Usenet, or FTP) and then either Stop or 1 of the remaining options. Using the Custom Search, you are allowed to set the order that Dog Pile will send your query out to the search engines from 1 through 23.

Highway 61
www.highway61.com

"Finally, a search for the 20th century!" is your greeting at this meta-searcher site. Your query is submitted to Alta Vista, Excite, Infoseek, Lycos, Webcrawler and Yahoo for responses. You're, however, allowed a few options such as using the Or or And Boolean terms.

Your Patience Level allows you to set your search pace (and returns). The options are:

- Hurry Up! You Losers!

- Please Try and Make It Quick!

- I'm a Reasonable Person

- Time is a Relative Thing...

- Take Your Time, I'm Going to the Bathroom

You have a choice of Lots (35 to 75) or Bury Me (60 to 125) for the number of hits returned. In truth, the returns were quite relevant and included a rank based on how many sites a link was found at and how those sites ranked it.

Savvy Search
guaraldi.cs.colostate.edu:2000

This is an "Experimental search system" that searches 25 search engines databases simultaneously for your hits. You can request that the hits contain All Query Terms, All Query Terms As A Phrase or Any Query Term.

You can also specify that it displays results in a Brief, Normal or Verbose format. The returns were quite relevant to the search. Be aware, however, that these meta searches can take a little bit longer to display your hits. An interesting bonus of this site is that it is offered in 22 languages besides English.

search.onramp.net
search.onramp.net

This meta-search site queries A2Z, Excite, Hotbot, Infoseek, Lycos, Ultra, Webcrawler and Yahoo and correlates the results of the different search engines into a single list.

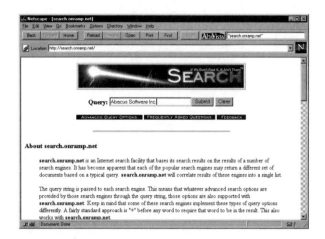

They suggest using "+" before any word that is required to be in the results. The Advanced query option allows you to give Max Delay (maximum seconds allowed to wait for each search engine) and Max Results (maximum number of results to display), with the Configure Weights the most interesting.

Of the eight search engines, you can assign a weight to each search engine. That weight is multiplied by the point value that is normally associated with each result. For example, if you set the weight at 3, then the number one result from that search engine would get 30 points for the score.

If you set the value to zero, it disables that search engine for the search. No query would then be sent to it. This sounds more difficult than it is but don't let this discourage you from trying it.

Specialized search engines to organize information

To organize information on certain subjects better, more specialized search engines will start to emerge. These search engines collect and often review sites that are relevant to a particular subject. They've essentially done all the initial foot work for you. This saves you time because you won't need to sort through several general search engines for all the information they have already cataloged.

Along with search options, most will have other information that is relevant to your subject or industry. If you're having problems finding these, try associations or trade magazines for assistance. The following lists a few of the specialized search engines.

AstroWeb
www.stsci.edu/astroweb/astronomy.html

This database is maintained by the AstroWeb Consortium – nine individuals at seven institutions – and contains 2436 distinct resource records. You can use a search option or go directly to sections within the nine main categories. They include:

- ➢ Observing Resources

- ➢ Data Resources

- ➢ Publication-Related Resources

- ➢ Organizations

- ➢ Software Resources

- ➢ Research Areas of Astronomy

- ➢ Astronomical Imagery

- ➢ Miscellaneous Resources

- ➢ Various Lists of Astronomy Resources

If you're using the Search option, be aware that OR is the default search term. You can also use AND, NOT or (*) for partial words.

HealthAtoZ
www.healthatoz.com

The Overview section of this site reads "HealthAtoZ aspires to be your Internet navigation tool and information resource in health and medicine." That's a good summary of their objective.

Your basic query can search All or Any Keywords Entered and will search either Reviewed Sites or the Entire Database (your choice). The Advanced Search allows for Any or All of the Keywords, at either a Partial or Exact Match.

You can also specify the number of documents (from 10 - 100) that will display the results in Compact or Standard Form.

You can chose from among 27 categories, including:

- ➤ Allied Health
- ➤ Emergency Care & Services
- ➤ Managed Care
- ➤ Veterinary Medicine

- ➤ Alternative Medicine
- ➤ Journals & Periodicals
- ➤ Pharmaceuticals & Drugs
- ➤ Women's Health

StreetEYE
www.streeteye.com

They call themselves "...the definitive directory and search engine of Internet resources relevant to investors and investment professionals." The search option has an AND default but also accepts OR and NOT.

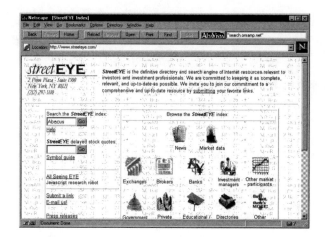

The following are also available at this site:

➤ Delayed Stock Quotes	➤ News Market Data
➤ Exchanges	➤ Brokers
➤ Banks	➤ Investment Managers
➤ Other Market Participants	➤ Government
➤ Private Services	➤ Educational/Nonprofit
➤ Directories of Links	➤ Other Resources
➤ Personal Finance	➤ Non-Financial Resources

Pay Dirt! (Good Sites For Information)

After spending several hours reviewing many sites, I have compiled a list of those sites that provide good links and those sites that have useful information for your CI search. As some of these addresses are within sites, make certain to enter the **exact** address as shown.

Serving up those links!

The following sites provide various links to other sites for more specific information. I like to think of them as "transfer" stations on the information highway.

AT&T Business Network Business Bookmarks
www.bnet.att.com

"The Home Page for Business" is the way AT&T is billing this site. In a joint-venture deal, Industry Net (www.industry.net) is now considered a sister site to this and does have a hyper link to it (more on Industry Net later).

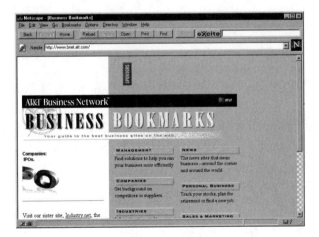

The Business Bookmarks include:

> Management
> Companies

> Industries
> Government

> News
> Personal Business

> Sales & Marketing
> Regional Resources

The Management section has coverage on:

> Starting a Business
> Corporate Finance

> Human Resources
> Legal

> Improving Production
> Office Administration

> Technology

The Companies section has Company Profiles. This includes links for:

> Company Listings

> Company Culture

> Public & Private Firms information

> More Financial Information

Most of the information from the Company profile section are fee-based services, including Dunn & Bradstreet and Avenue Technologies. News, SEC Data and Analysis are a few of the options listed under More Financial Information. Company Rankings – listed under Company Listings – includes links to many articles about the Top 500, Top 100, Up and Coming, etc.

You should definitely take a look at the Business Ethics heading under Company Culture. It includes links to:

➤ The Better Business Bureau

➤ Business Ethics Magazine

➤ KPMG Business Ethics Web Site

You can search in the Industries section by SIC Code Division or from an Alphabetic List. The Divisions include Agriculture, Construction, Manufacturing, Mining and Transportation.

Each of the industries listed has links to Directories, Organizations, Publications and Other.

The Government section includes Federal Government links as well as Hot Topics, Getting Government Business & Loans and State Governments. This is a good area to check out if you need to find government agencies in the states where your competitors are located, such as the Secretary of State, etc.

The News section includes:

➤ Hot Topics

➤ Management News

➤ Special Reports

➤ Marketing News

➤ Technology News

The headings you'll find within the Personal Business section include:

➤ Personal Finance

➤ Jobs & careers

➤ Travel

At the Regional Resources section you can access information such as:

➢ Chambers of Commerce Directories

➢ Government Sites

➢ Media/News

➢ Other State Resources for each state

Should you be looking into the competitors' areas, this would be worthwhile to stop by for a browse of what is available.

All-In-One's Search Page/World Wide Web
www.albany.net/allinone/all1www.html#WWW

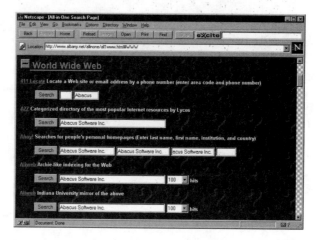

This section of All-In-One's Search Page site has links to over 50 search engines. Links include:

➢ A2Z

➢ AliWeb

➢ Ecola's Tech Directory

➢ Forum One

➢ I-Explorer

➢ LinkStar

➢ Look Smart

➢ Net Guide Live

➢ Rank Link

➢ RBSE's URL Database

Although you will need to query each one independently, All-In-One does provide easy access to a variety of engines that you may not ordinarily see.

The BUBL WWW Subject Tree - Alphabetical Arrangement
bubl.bath.ac.uk/link/subjects

BUBL (BUlletin Board for Libraries) has a combined Gopher and Web system containing links to resources that are relevant to the global LIS (Library Information Studies) community.

It has over 94 "subjects" listed, with examples such as:

➤ Accounting	➤ Architecture
➤ Banking	➤ Chemical Engineering
➤ Dentistry	➤ Environment
➤ Mechanical Engineering	➤ Medicine
➤ Pharmacy	➤ Publishing & Bookselling
➤ Textiles	➤ Veterinary Medicine
➤ Zoology	➤ Government & Public Administration

The Business section is definitely worth the trip (for this purpose) as it includes:

➤ General Resources	➤ Centres & Projects
➤ Journals	➤ Magazines
➤ Directories	➤ Small Business
➤ Entrepreneurship	

Depending on your industry or business, you'll find many sites to go to from this section. As with many of these sites, be patient and don't panic when you see the long list. Each includes very accurate descriptions so you only have to travel where it looks as if you should.

Business Information Sources on the Internet
dis.strath.ac.uk/business

This page is within the University of Strathclyde's home page (dis.strath.ac.uk/). Based out of Glasgow, Scotland, I was quite skeptical of this site when I heard of it. However, after you visit this site, you'll see that many of the sites pertain to US markets and the descriptions are very good.

It's also one of the most current sites I have visited with updates performed monthly. Sheila Webber is the contact person for this section if you have questions. She's very prompt in her responses.

This section is broken down to:

> Fashion Net

> Used Equipment Network

> Search Engines

> Reviews of Search Engines

> Search the Descriptions of this Site

> Other Guides to Internet Business Sources (includes: Krislyn's Strictly Business Site, A Business Researchers Interest, Rutgers University Business Resources and WWW Virtual Library)

> Company Directories (UK & North America and Worldwide & Other Countries)

> Trade Industry (includes: Fisher Scientific, Gas & Oil Pipeline Information and Ply-Links)

➤ Company Profiles and Financial Information (includes: Berkshire Online Edgar and Fortune)

➤ Country Information Market, Statistical and Economic News Sources (includes AJR Newslink, News Alert, American City Business Journals and Business Week Online)

➤ News Sources Published in the UK

➤ Discussion Lists: examples include Electronic Bulletins and Current Awareness and Keeping Up-To-Date with New Web Sites.

It may take you a few days to get through just this section (but it's time well spent).

Clark Net's Awesome Resources
www.clark.net/pub/journalism/awesome.html#top

An Internet service for Maryland, DC and Northern Virginia, this section of the site has 47 Truly Awesome and 99 Awesome links to sites. Within the Truly Awesome list are links to:

➤ College and University Home Pages

➤ Deja News   ➤ The Federal Web Locator

➤ InfoSpace   ➤ MapQuest

➤ Planet Earth   ➤ Virtual Medical Center

The Awesome sites include links to:

➤ Amazon Books

➤ A Business Researcher's Internet

➤ The Electronic Newstand

➤ Four11

➢ InterNIC Directory and database Services

➢ Library of Congress

➢ Medscape

➢ PharmInfoNet

➢ Scholarly Journals

➢ Thomas Register of America

➢ Trade Show Central

➢ WWW Yellow Pages.

You'll probably recognize some of them but others you'll have to visit just to see where you end up (unfortunately, descriptions are not included).

Clearinghouse's Business & Employment
www.clearinghouse.net/cgi-bin/chadmin/viewcat/
Business_Employment?kywd++

The Argus Clearinghouse site, self billed as a "The Premier Internet Research Library," has a total of 12 categories from which to choose. For the purposes here, the Business & Employment category provides a several useful links.

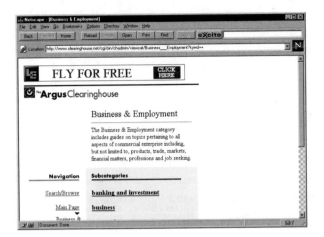

There are eight subcategories from which to choose. They include:

- Banking & Investment
- Business
- Economics
- Employment
- Finance & Credit
- Human Resources
- Industry
- Marketing

The Business subsection has:

- Agribusiness
- Business Directories
- Companies
- Franchises
- Meeting & Event Planning
- Retailing
- TQM

The Industry section has, among others:

- Airlines
- Breweries
- Chemical Industry
- Farming

> Fire Protection   ➢ Marine Industry

> Oil & Gas Industry   ➢ Steel

> Winery   ➢ Wool

FINWEB
www.finweb.com

This Internet resource is self billed as "A Financial Economics WWW Server." This site provides many links to sites dedicated to financial information, including many forecasts for different industries. The Database includes:

> Edgar Online

> Holt's Stock Market Reports

> Merrill Lynch

> QuoteCom

> Federal Deposit Insurance Corporation

The Electronic Publishing links include:

> Journal of Finance

> Net Exposure

> Review of Economic Studies

> Financial Executive Journal

> Resources for Economists on the Internet

Find Links
www.findlinks.com/index.html

The "Industry-Specific World Wide Web News, Links and Classifieds" site from Find Links out of Santa Cruz, CA offers 9 different Industry Links (from Agriculture to Petroleum), with four other industry links "Coming Soon."

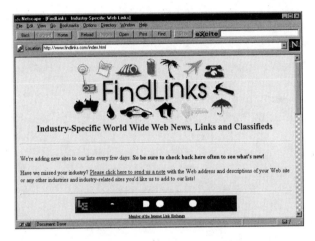

Each of these 9 Industries have the following categories with which to link to other sites:

- ➢ Index
- ➢ Associations
- ➢ Classified Ads
- ➢ Related Companies & Suppliers
- ➢ News, Magazines & Journals
- ➢ Information, Research, & Education
- ➢ Companies
- ➢ Government
- ➢ Other Web Directories

Galaxy's Business and Commerce
galaxy.tradewave.com/galaxy/Business-and-Commerce.html

This site is a bit more involved than many sites you'll visit.

The Business and Commerce section includes:

➢ General Resources

➢ Consumer Products & Services
(with over 30 topics, including Automobiles, Building & Remodeling, Legal, Safety, Yard & Garden)

➢ General Products & Services
(over 70 topics listed here, including: Aerospace, Biotechnology, Commercial Printers, Energy, Industrial Design, Manufacturing, Packaging and Trophies & Awards)

Business General Resources has 5 sections for every listing that includes information found by:

➢ Articles

➢ Collections

➢ Commercial Organizations

➢ Government Organizations

➢ Periodicals

It also includes Product & Service Descriptions.

This site also includes Collections (i.e., The Business Clearinghouse and Interesting Business Sites on the Web) and Directories (i.e., Business Resources - Babson College, Go M-Link/Business Collection and Texas A & M/Business Collection).

Industry Home Pages
www.virtualpet.com/industry/mfg/mfg.htm>:

There are 33 industries represented within the US Industry home pages that include Aerospace/Aviation, Building & Construction, Coatings, Fitness, Food & Beverage and Hotel & Lodging.

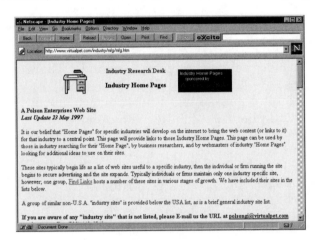

There are also sections for Industry Home Pages Outside the USA and General Industry Pages. As you will note, there are some industries listed above that are not "common" for such sites, so you may well want to check out this site.

Industry Link
www.industrylink.com

This is a directory of links to industry web sites. You can search the directory database by filing out a form to include (all or any) company name, URL, state/province, country, industry and description.

As you can also search by industry, some of those include:

> Automation

> Electronics

> Measurement & Control

> Plastics & Polimers

> Heavy Equipment & Machinery

When searching by industry, you'll receive a listing that includes both reference and commercial sites, each as such designated.

Internet Sleuth/Internet - Web Search Engines
www.isleuth.com/webs.html

What a place to look for search engines! There are links to over 20 separate search engines here that include:

> Cyberhound   > Inktomi

> Jump City   > Link Monster

> Magellan   > NlightN

> Spectre Searcher   > USE IT

> WWW Worm

As different search engines produce different results, and not all are as widely known as others, sites such as this one give you an opportunity to access those that you may not have even heard of before.

LSU's Internet Business Resource Page
www.lib.lsu.edu/weblio.html#Business

This is located within the Louisiana State University's Virtual Library, "Webliography." It has eight categories from which to select. The Business & Industry News category includes:

> Economic & Corporate Research Reports
  (Briefings & Indicators Economic & Financial Markets and Word from Wall Street)

➤ Industries
(Air Transport Association, Communications, Industries Report, Industry Features, National Restaurant Association, Retail Industry Profile and Utilities)

➤ International

➤ Local, Regional & State

➤ National

➤ Periodicals

➤ Public Policy

MSU School of Criminal Justice
SCIP Project's Domestic Links
ssc.msu.edu/~cj/domlinks.html

This site offers links that cater to the CI function. This page is divided into five sections:

➤ Case Law

➤ General

➤ Government Offices

➤ Organizations

➤ Periodicals

A few examples of the links include: Intellectual Property: General, U.S. House of Representatives Internet Law Library and the Library of Congress under Case Law. General has links to Intellectual Property Center and Strategic Intelligence. Government Offices can get you to

U.S. Patent & Trademark Offices, Department of Commerce and FBI ANSIR. So far, the World Intellectual Property Organization is the only Organization listed. Intellectual Property Magazine and Intellectual Property Worldwide are currently the only periodicals here.

Manufacturing Process Home Pages
www.virtualpet.com/industry/process/process.htm

Here, there are 12 specific manufacturing processes from which to choose:

- ➤ Die Casting
- ➤ Logistics
- ➤ Metal Finishing
- ➤ Metal Working
- ➤ Paint/Coatings
- ➤ Welding
- ➤ Joining
- ➤ Metal Fabrication
- ➤ Metal Treating
- ➤ Packaging
- ➤ Construction Resin

These all have at least one site to which you can link.

Nijenrode Business Webserver's Business Related Collections and Directories
www.nijenrode.nl/nbr/collections/

This is part of the Netherlands Business School web site at Nijenrode University. This is an excellent collection of business-related links where about 90% are resources for businesses in the United States. There are over 20 resource links listed here. They include:

- ➤ Business & Economic Resources
- ➤ Thomas Ho's Favorite Electronic Commerce WWW Resources
- ➤ Hoovers Online

➢ World Class

➢ Online Quality Resource Guide

Resource Connection
www.edgeonline.com/main/resourcepage/

This is the Resource section of the Entrepreneurial Edge Online site (www.edgeonline.com). It features 16 subcategories that range from Associations and Banking to Stock Market, Software and Internet Services. While each subcategory has great links, you should look into the following for CI purposes:

➢ Small Business

➢ Education

➢ Associations

➢ Legal

➢ Resource Indexes
(This site is specifically geared for entrepreneurs)

Other sections include:

➢ Edge Magazine

➢ Business Builders

➢ Interactive Toolbox

➢ SmallbizNet

U.S. Business Advisor
www.business.gov

"The one-stop electronic link to government for business" is the opening line of this site. Operated and monitored by the National Technical Information Service, it's a very useful site with links to every government agency you may consider and then some. It provides accurate descriptions of each agency or service to which you're about to proceed. It notifies you when leaving the US Advisor site for other sites and even thanks you for visiting.

You're able to get information in five ways from the following subsections:

➢ Common Questions

➢ How To Search

➢ How To Browse

➢ News

At Common Questions, you are given eight sets of common questions and answers organized by subject. Those eight sets are listed as:

➤ Exports   ➤ Get Information (FCC)

➤ Search Federal Jobs (OPM)   ➤ Social Security

➤ Common Questions (OSHA)   ➤ Postal Service

➤ Small Business (SBA)   ➤ Taxes

If you cannot find what you're looking for, then it suggests that you try How to.... Here you'll find the tools and forms to help solve problems and do business with the government. These are listed in different areas:

➤ Address and Package Your Mail (USPS)

➤ Business Forms (USPS)

➤ Disaster Assistance (SBA)

➤ Do Business with GSA (GSA)

➤ Expand a Business (SBA)

➤ Finance a Business (SBA)

➤ FinanceNet (NPR)

➤ Get a Passport (DOS)

➤ Get a Service Corps of Retired Executives Counseling Appointment (SBA)

➤ Get a Small Business Innovation and Research (SBIR) and Small Business Technology transfer Research (SBA)

➤ Get GBD Leads and Useful Business News Information (SBA)

➤ Get Employer's Quick Reference Guide to Social Security (SSA)

> Get Forms and Directory of Small Business Lending from SBA (SBA)

> Get Forms and Publications from the IRS (IRS)

> Get Information on EPS's Partners for the Environment Program (EPA)

> Get Information on SBIR/STTR Awards (SBA)

> How Do I File W-2 Wage & Tax Statement (SSA)

> Make Your Building Compliant with Asbestos Rules (OSHA)

> Search EDGAR (SEC)

> Search Federal Jobs (OPM)

> Start a Business (SBA)

> Zip Code Lookup (USPS)

Now, if you still have not found what you were looking for, try Search. Here, you find on-line resources and regulations that may be of interest to you. These 5 areas include:

> Search On-Line Government Information

> Search Health, Safety and Environmental Regulations

> Search GPO's Databases of Congressional and Executive Branch Material

> Search Regulations in Development

> Search FinanceNet

Still not found what you wanted? Try Browse, which has 6 areas for information and services available from federal agencies, arranged by subject. These include:

➤ Doing Business with Government

➤ Finance

➤ General Business (this is probably the section with the most useful information/links regarding business at this site)

➤ International Trade

➤ Labor and Employment

➤ Laws and Regulations

Finally, there is News where you will find news releases from agencies of interest to the business community with links to other News Items.

A Business Compass
www.abcompass.com

Although this site bills itself as a "next-generation search engine", we're including it here because it's a good source of business-related sites.

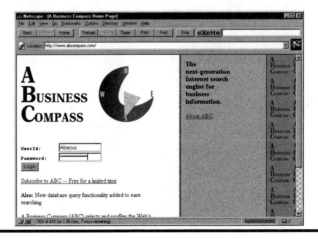

You can search by three categories:

- Subject

- Industry

- Geography

There are eight headings listed for Subjects. There are 44 listed for Industry and they include:

➢ Agriculture

➢ Architecture/Design

➢ Facilities Management

➢ Manufacturing

➢ Textiles & Clothing

➢ Transportation/Shipping

Geography offers seven regions and World. All the sites that are listed have a brief review that includes the hyperlink, it's intended Business Use, a Content Description, the Special Features and Valuable Pages within the site.

Wall Street Research Net
www.wsrn.com

While this site is said to contain over 190,000 links to assist investors — professional and private — in basic research on actively traded companies, many of the links are useful for privately held businesses for industry and economic information.

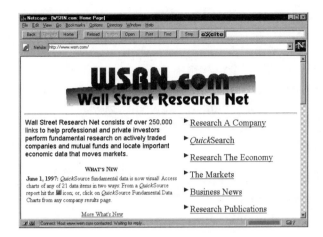

The sections include:

➢ Research a Company

➢ QuickSearch

➢ Research the Economy

➢ The Markets

➢ Business News

➢ Research Publications

➢ Mutual Funds

➢ Brokers & Services

Research the Economy includes links under:

➢ US Department of Commerce   ➢ US Courts

➢ Federal Reserve   ➢ Economic Research

➢ International Research   ➢ Government Links

Business News, Business Publications and Research Publications would be useful to anyone in business.

Business News includes links for News, Newspapers, Business Publications, Online Publications, and Other Information. And, Research Publications includes links for Economic Publications, Equity Publications, Market Resources, and Trade Associations & Other Groups.

Information gold mine

Now that the sites with links have been reviewed and you have been checking those out, it is time to review sites that contain specific information – destination sites.

AEC InfoCenter
www.aecinfo.com

This site acts as a business center for the Architecture, Engineering and Building Construction industries. With such sections as Building Products, Support Services, Interactive Forums, SpecCenter (TM), and Government & Authorities, this is well organized and contains good, useful information for those interested. They have also included feature articles, classifieds and project information.

College Net's College Search
www.collegenet.com/cgi-bin/
Webdriver?MIval=search_choices

This site is obviously designed for people interested in pursuing higher education. It's also, however, a very handy site to look up colleges and universities located near your competitor(s). As we hope you remember, it's always wise to check with area colleges or others offering programs specific to your industry in case any of the competitors have engaged in research or product development projects with these institutions.

At the "search" section of the site, you can search Four Year Schools and Community, Technical, and Junior Colleges by state. Most of the schools listed even have links right to their home pages so that you can pursue your query!

Deja News
www.dejanews.com

Since this site claims to have over 100 million articles on file, it's probably the best, and easiest way, to search the Usenet newsgroups.

As we mentioned, these groups are good not only for monitoring what is being said about you and your competitors, but also possible issues facing your industry and customers.

Searches at this site can be performed using a few different criteria such as the Quick Search that searches Usenet for specific keywords. Power Search offers lots of search options for advanced searches.

Query Filter allows you to filter for certain newsgroups, dates, authors and subjects. The Query Profile option searches the newsgroups where your keyword(s) appear most often. Don't be afraid to use the extensive Help section for each option.

E-Mail Discussion Groups
www.nova.edu/Inter-Links/listserv.html

This site offers a few different options for searching listserv mailing lists. Your options at the Finding a list section include:

➢ Directory of Scholarly E-Lists

➢ Inter-Links Search for Discussion Groups

➢ Liszt Directory of E-Mail Discussion Groups

➢ Search the List of Lists

➢ Tile.net List of Internet Discussion Groups

The other section, Help Files, includes mail list manager commands and some general information about listservs. Now there's no reason to miss being on the mailing lists relevant to your industry/business.

Forbes 49th Annual Report on American Industry
www.forbes.com/forbes/97/0113/5901092a.htm

This is an annual report Forbes Magazine publishes on a select group of industries. Twenty industries were tracked for this report, including:

➢ Aerospace & Defense

➢ Travel & Transport

➢ Capital Goods

➢ Chemicals

➢ Energy

➢ Food, Drink & Tobacco

➢ Metals

➢ Retailing

A Profitability and Growth chart can be accessed that outlines each industry's performance for the past five years. Within each industry category, you're able to access a report that lists how many and what companies were surveyed for the report, and to see how each fared within the industry and against each other.

Hot Tips of the Day
www.smartbiz.com/sbs/hottips.htm

This is a section of the Smart Business Supersite (www.smartbiz.com) that offers "hot tips" every business day. I was able to find "How to start your computer consulting business" under General Business Tips from Entrepreneur on my first try.

The other categories include:

➤ Saving Money Tips From SBS

➤ Computer Q & A From Kim Komando

➤ Management Tips From SBS

➤ Business Travel Tips From SBS

This section has archives of tips from past months, too, so you won't be too "cold" for some time!

InfoSpace - the Ultimate Directory
www.infospace.com

When it comes to verifying address information for your competitors, this site is one of the best places to start. In the Yellow Pages section, you can search Businesses by Category or Businesses by Name.

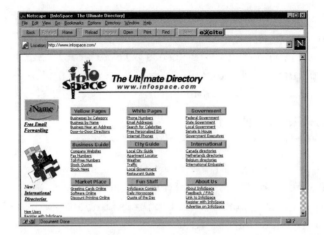

We should mention that you may want to only enter the company name and state for your search criteria. The specific city – as you know it – may be incorrect if the official listing is a suburb of the city you know.

It also includes sections for Government and International searches.

Industry Trade Publications
ecola.com/news/magazine/industry

This site has over 80 magazine links listed that include:

➢ Canmaker	➢ Forging
➢ Futon Life	➢ Gear Technology
➢ Imprint	➢ Inside Self-Storage
➢ Pest Control Technology	➢ Plastics News
➢ Waste News	➢ Rug News
➢ Security	➢ Sports Trends
➢ A & E - Awards & Engraving	
➢ American Metal Market	

> Manufacturing Systems

> Nation's Restaurant News

> Professional Carwashing & Detailing

There are also 14 industry trade publications for countries other than the US that include Australia, Hong Kong, India, Italy, South Africa, and the United Kingdom.

Industry.Net
www.industry.net

Self billed as "Where Industry Does Business", this site has a lot of information on the companies that are listed here. First, note that you will have to register to retrieve any specific information, but this is a free service (you simply provide them with some information).

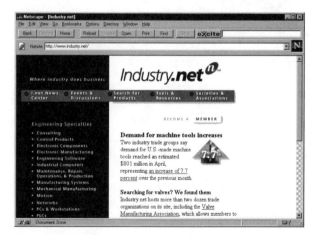

Although companies must pay to be represented on this site, product information, company information and more is available. This site is searchable by Product/Service, Company or Manufacturer. It also has very comprehensive news links and stories on the various industries represented on this site (at the i.net News Center section).

The Events & Discussion section includes Business & Industry Internet Newsgroups. With over 60 newsgroups from which to choose, everyone who visits this site (related to your industry) should be able to find a group or two. These include:

- ➢ alt.business.misc

- ➢ alt.industrial

- ➢ comp.cad.i-deas

- ➢ comp.robotics.misc

- ➢ misc.jobs

- ➢ misc.legal

- ➢ sci.chem

- ➢ sci.energy

- ➢ sci.polymers

There are over 25 links at the Societies & Associations section to various sites. These sites include:

- ➢ Association for Manufacturing Excellence (AME)

- ➢ Casting Industry Suppliers Association (CISA)

- ➢ Industrial Fasteners Institute (IFI)

- ➢ Metal Treating Institute (MTE)

- ➢ Valve Manufacturers Association (VMA)

The Monster Board
www.monsterboard.com

This site claims to have over 50,000 jobs posted and over 100,000 resumes on file. Now, as one way to monitor your competitors' activities, it has been suggested that you look out for job postings. You can even review about 4,000 Employer Profiles of the leading corporations worldwide (who knows who may be listed).

You can search newsgroups by keywords or you can use Jabba-the-Hunt for searching their database of job postings by location, discipline, or keyword. Of course, this is not to say that your competitors are using the Internet for such matters.

NASDAQ
www.nasdaq.com

This site is very easy to use and has quite a bit of information beyond what you may expect. Besides Full Quote, there is Most Active (which includes a few other interesting lists), and even Market News. While reported in short form, it is easy to read and it reports on virtually all the markets.

National Bureau of Economic Research
www.nber.org

This private nonprofit, nonpartisan organization has been around for about 70 years. Its sole focus is economic information, both historical (covering 150 years) and current.

The NBER web site is organized into:

> ➤ Macro Data

> ➤ Industry Data

> ➤ Individual Data

123

Listings and analysis of business cycle dates are available from the NBER Official Business Cycles Dates section under Macro Data. They have the Bartelsman & Gray Manufacturing Industry Productivity Database that contains annual production and cost data for several manufacturing industries from 1958 to 1991. There is also a searchable index of NBER working papers.

This site is obviously a necessity if you're looking for historical information for your industry. It may also be a good place to find experts in your industry.

Newsletter Access
www.newsletter.access

This site has an international directory of over 5000 newsletters for just about anyone, including business professionals. There are about 62 subjects from which to choose that include:

➢ Advertising

➢ Aviation & Eurospace

➢ Chemicals

➢ Furniture

➢ Machinery

➢ Science

➢ Transportation

As these are just links to information for the newsletters – and probably all have fees – it did seem to be an easy way to see what newsletters were available and to then contact them direct.

Publicly Accessible Mailing Lists
www.neosoft.com/internet/paml

Courtesy of NeoSoft, this is a list of mailing lists available through the Internet and the UUCP network. Mailing lists were discussed as a means of monitoring what the public is saying about your competitors and your company.

This version of the list is updated a few days after the Usenet version is posted (which is around the end of each month). You'll see a message if your list is more than one month old because the group listings are continuously changing. Therefore, you may want to check in around the first of the month for the new listings.

Society of Competitive Intelligence Professionals
www.scip.org

This group of CI professionals was formed in 1986. It was, and still is, an effort to help professionals in this field and to further CI education. Here, you can learn more about the organization and its membership benefits.

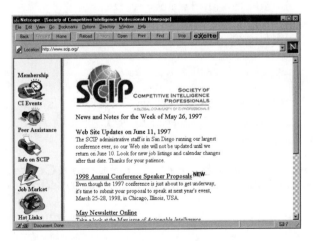

The Peer Assistance section includes:

➢ Experts & Speaker database

➢ Competitive Intelligence Forums

➢ The Job Marketplace

➢ Association Resource Links

➢ Curriculum Modules for Educational Programs

The Publications section includes:

➢ The SCIP Web Journal

➢ Actional Intelligence (online newsletter)

➢ Competitive Intelligence Review

The Surveys & Data section includes:

➢ Global Survey of CI

➢ Lund University Survey

➢ Intelligence Systems Software Survey

➢ SCIP Web Statistics

Currently, the 1997 Directory lists SCIP's members plus it has a resource section that includes CI Consultants and Vendors of Information Services.

Small Business Advancement National Center Industry Profiles
www.sbaer.uca.edu/sbaer/Publications/index.html#industry

This particular link from the SBANC home page (www.sbaer.uca.edu) has 33 reports on industries from Advertising and Antique Shops to Subdividers and Typing Services. What makes these reports so useful are sections such as:

➤ General Industry Information

➤ Market Opportunities

➤ Costs & Financial Considerations

➤ Typical Business Ratios for Firms in the Industry

➤ Management Considerations

➤ Development & Site Locations

I was quite impressed by the industries that were listed; some were rather unusual and, I would suspect, it was probably difficult to find detailed information about these industries.

Thomas Food Industry Register
www.tfir.com:80/index-new.html

This site is for those seeking information on the food industry in the US. This site claims to have more than 30,000 US and Canadian suppliers of food products, ingredients, equipment and supplies listed under 6,000 product categories. You can also get information on trade shows for this industry.

The Government Resources is a huge listing of several government agencies and offices for assistance in about every area you can think of for food. The Food Trends section is very useful in that it has current and previous survey results and reports that include general trends within certain segments, specific product categories and market studies on specific industries.

This database search is driven by a request for a product/service or company name. A location (state/province) can be specified along with either.

Thomas Register of American Manufacturers
www.thomasregister.com

This site is obviously for those looking for information on manufacturing in the US. They claim to have 155,000 companies in their database with 55,000 product and service classifications. Also, they have over 3,100 online supplier catalogs that total about 42,000 detailed pages of buying and specifying information.

The search is driven by a request for information on a particular product/service or a company name. You can specify location (state/province) for both. A "C" indicates that the company has an online catalog and an "F" indicates that the company has literature available by fax.

There are also links to other Thomas Publishing sites, professional sites (Thomas AutoDesk Data Publishing and PartSpec Online), and a few Industry and Trade Associations. It should be noted that this site is not as comprehensive as the traditional printed version of The Thomas Register.

Yahoo's Professional Organizations
www.yahoo.com/Economy/Organizations/Professional

This section of Yahoo lists about 68 organizations. The American Management Association, Chemical Resources & Management Association, ClubNet, International Marina Institute, National Spa & Pool Foundation and the Society of Fund Raising Executives are just a few of the links here. Many good contacts and experts may be found in these links, so see if your industry is represented!

National Institute of Standards and Technology
www.nist.gov

Originally formed as the National Bureau of Standards in 1901 to support industry, commerce, scientific institutions and all branches of the government, it became the NIST 1989. NIST comprises 4 major programs:

➤ Advanced Technology Program (ATP)

➤ Manufacturing Extensions Partnership (MEP)

➤ Laboratory Research and Services

➤ Baldridge National Quality Program

The site offers such information as News, Programs, Products and Services, Search and even Other WWW Links.

An Index of NIST's Technical Activities (TA) is available in the Search section. It includes brief mission statements for all the NIST research groups, along with contact names, e-mail addresses and telephone numbers.

Some of the TAs include Biochemistry, Ceramics, Computer Systems and Manufacturing.

The Other WWW Links section offers Federal Links, Professional Organizations, and Other Interesting links. If you're looking for a professional organization, try this link – there are at least 30 listed here.

Remember our discussion of experts and cultivating relationships? Look here to see if your industry is represented and start those contacts.

U.S. Chamber of Commerce
www.uschamber.com

As you may know, the Chamber of Commerce was created to assist business to act as a sort of go-between for the government and business.

Their site has sections that include:

➤ Broadcasting

➤ Chamber Mall

➤ Issue Information

➤ Membership

➤ News & Media Releases

➤ Programs & Training

➤ Publications

➤ Small Business Resources

➤ What's New

As the Chamber can offer such information as demographics, they can also help keep you abreast of some of the issues facing small businesses and how to address them.

Bureau of Labor Statistics
stats.bls.gov/blshome.html

We mentioned in the U. S. Business Advisor information that this site should not be overlooked. As is typical of the government, this is not the easiest site to understand. However, once you become familiar with the site, you'll find a lot of information.

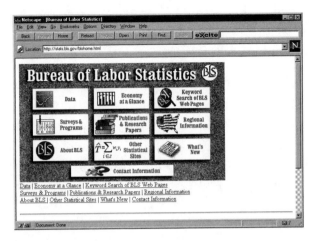

This includes reports on about any industry you can consider:

➤ Labor Force Statistics

➤ Consumer Price Indexes

➤ Producer Price Indexes

Reports within the Surveys & Programs include:

➤ Employment & Unemployment

➤ Prices & Living Conditions

➤ Compensation & Working Conditions

➤ Productivity & Technology

Reports in the Economy at a Glace section include:

➤ Civilian Labor Force

➤ Unemployment

➤ Average Weekly Hours

➤ Average Weekly Earnings

➤ Productivity reports for the past 12 months

United States Patent and Trademark Office
www.uspto.gov

This is a great site. Although another site is on the Internet that will perform patent searches for you, it charges a fee. Not only can you search for existing patents and trademarks, but you can also register your product, etc. at this site (forms available by downloading them).

A fee is charged to apply for the registration but no fee is charged for the searches. There are also a lot of reports on about anything that has to do with patents and trademarks. There are even links to offices similar to this in many other countries. You can get a multinational trademark without leaving your computer.

The U S Census Bureau/The Official Statistics
www.census.gov

This site contains great census information and is very comprehensive and full of historical information. The News section has very pertinent information. Access Tools includes the following:

➤ Interactive Software

➤ Browse All Public Directories & Files

➤ Download Software

➤ Census Data Tools at Other Sites

Let's see, Subjects A - Z...what were you expecting here? This is what it is!! Search has a few different options to by which to search.

Current Economic Indicators includes:

> About Business

> About People

> Tools & Tidbets

> Data Elsewhere

Industry, Trade and Technology Review
www.usitc.gov/ittr.htm

From the Office of Industries, this site is for the Industry, Trade, and Technology Review, a quarterly publication. It's intended to provide analysis of issues and insights into the global position of U.S. industries, their technological competitiveness, and the implications of trade and policy developments to these industries. You can either search this site or browse whatever path you choose.

Extra! Extra! Read all about it!

As news sources play a role in CI research, the following are sites with links to various news sources and actual sites of those major sources. Depending on the information you are looking for, you may want to scan several sources or focus on a particular one.

Business Wire
www.businesswire.com

This is a very organized site that is easy to navigate. First, it provides up to the minute news at Today's News on the Net that is updated every hour. This site also offers High-Tech Link and Health Link for anyone interested in those industries. Corporate News on the Net is searchable by company name or industry.

The Corporate Profile section is searchable by company name. Business Wire also offers a few fee-based services such as CompetitorTrak, IndustryTrak, and NetClips. CompetitorTrak is a continuous 24-hour service that tracks news releases from Business Wire and First Call Corporate Release based on keywords (industries, companies, products or developments) that you select.

IndustryTrak is a service that tracks news and information on 24 key industries (Apparel/Textiles, Energy/Utilities and Metals/Mining & Mineral Resources are a few) with such sources as First Call Corporate Services, Ziff-Davis Interactive, Intell.X/Data Times, Knight-Ridder Business/Tribune News, and American Banker.

The headlines are divided by major news categories: by earnings, dividends, mergers & acquisitions, product announcements, management changes, advisories, and other news.

NetClips is a service that performs weekly searches of the more than 16,000 newsgroups on the Internet for keywords you have chosen and then sends the headlines to you.

CNN Interactive
www.cnn.com

While this site is not necessarily aimed at business news, it does have U.S and World news sections. The Sci-Tech and Health categories were quite good in that they had actual content articles. So anyone in these industries would want to check out this area.

An interesting section, however, is Newsmakers. It has a searchable database of profiles on individuals, with such headings as Business Leaders, U.S. Newsmakers and World Newsmakers.

Editor & Publisher's Online Newspapers
www.mediainfo.com/ephome/npaper/nphtm/online.htm

This is a directory of online newspapers from all over the world. The site states that there are a total of 1692 newspapers listed online. There are a total of nine regions listed with the United States as one.

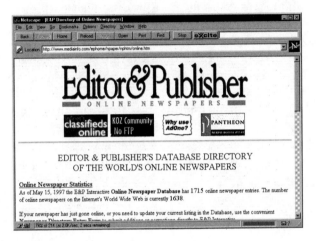

News Page
www.newspage.com

This site has 21 categories by which to "browse the news." The Business Management and Company Tracking were generally the most useful. However, depending on your industry, one of the other 19 sites will most likely contain more specific news for you.

Business Management includes:

➢ General Business Developments

➢ Business Management

➢ Human Resource Issues

➢ Sales & Marketing

➢ Finance Management

➤ General Economic & Trade Issues

➤ Financial Services & Investments

➤ Information Technology for Business

➤ Telecommunications for Business

Under the first subcategory, there were Executive Personnel Changes, Company Mergers & Acquisitions, etc. The companies listed under Company Tracking are primarily public-held companies.

Also be aware that some articles require you to pay a fee. The amount is posted at each article that has a charge. The cost is quite minimal, but nonetheless, there is a transaction involved. You may be able to get the source and peruse it from another venue or even gleam enough information from the "teaser" so that you don't have to pursue the rest of the article.

News Source
www.newo.com/news

This section of this site is dedicated to new sources all over the world. You can search for these sources by a Location or Keyword search. The Location option allows you to search by geography for Africa, Asia & Oceania, Europe, North America, and South & Central America. Within each of these, it is broken down by specific countries, or in the case of the USA, by states.

There is also a listing of about 20 specific news source links that include the Christian Science Monitor and CNN World News to USA Today World News and View from the Pacific – JINN Magazine.

It's definitely a place to check out for local publications when tracking the competitor's local news!

Newspaper Association of America's Hotlinks
www.naa.org/hot/index.html

OK, remember when we discussed scanning or subscribing to newspapers and even business journals in the towns of your competitors? Well, now you may be able to do that online. This site, from the Newspaper Association of America, has links that include U.S Dailies, Canadian Newspapers, Selected International Papers, Weeklies, Business papers, and Alternative Press.

This is a site to check out as I promise that you will be surprised at the newspapers listed. It's also much easier to read here than having to wait for it in the mail.

PR Newswire
www.prnewswire.com

This site is well organized and contains some very useful information. Some of the categories include:

➢ Company News

➢ Industry Focus

➢ Links

➢ Today's News

We hope they'll add more industries to the focus, but for now it includes:

➢ Automotive

➢ Energy

➢ Entertainment

➢ Financial

➢ Health/Biotech

> Technology

> Washington (government, in other words)

Don't forget the New York Times Syndicate. The Links section includes U.S. and International Exchanges. Trust me on this and just visit the section; if I listed all the headings you would not go.

Reuters
www.reuters.com

"The Business of Information" is the slogan of one of the largest and most reputable news sources. While the basic news stories are presented well and are free, the customized and specific information services – aimed primarily at the financial, media, and professional markets – are fee-based.

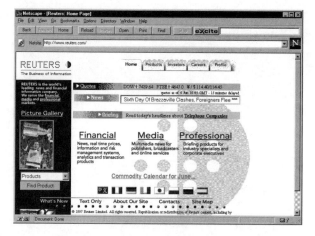

Never one to rule anything out completely, you should review the services available for the markets listed as you may find the price worth the accuracy and the time saved.

10

Other Methods To This Madness

Other Methods To This Madness

In seeing how bogged down people can get with so much information, and not always enough time to find it all, companies are looking for ways to assist you in the searching and updating of information at the sites that you regularly monitor.

Although some are just extensions of services already available, there are some technologies available that will make it much easier to get the information you need when you need it.

Roll It And Stamp It For Me

As search engines and information sites look to add to their existing services, you'll see a lot more of the personalized information options available. They save time and a lot of frustration in sorting through all the sites and files on the Internet that just may not be what you are looking for. As there are probably many more available, let's just review these for this part.

All these are currently offered at no charge (that's right – free!).

Excite Inc. My Excite Channel
www.excite.com

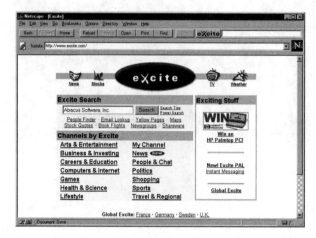

The sections for this are include the following:

➢ Front Page   ➢ Business

➢ Sports   ➢ Weather

➢ Entertainment   ➢ Lifestyle

➢ Technology   ➢ Nation-World

➢ Fun

Your Front Page has News listings that include 24 categories – many
of which are specific sports news - that include:

➢ Headline News   ➢ Business

➢ Technology   ➢ International

➢ Political

Favorite Links is included on the Front Page, where you can opt to include CNN, MSNBC, USA Today, LA Times and SF Chronicle along with specifying any of your favorite URLs. News Tracker covers the latest stories from over 300 of the web's top publications and allows you to customize your topics for specific company or industry information. At the Stock Portfolio section you can select which stocks to follow, along with links to the Most Active, Biggest Gainers and Biggest Losers.

Infoseek's Personalized News
www.infoseek.com

The sections for this are:

> ➢ Personalized News (World, Business, Technology, and Stocks)

> ➢ General News (Top News, World, Business, Technology, Sports, Politics and Entertainment)

> ➢ Personalized Info (Weather, Movies, TV Listings, Cartoons, and Horoscope)

For each of the sections, you enter the topics or keywords that you want to track (not from a form).

Yahoo Inc. My Yahoo
www.yahoo.com

The sections for this are:

> ➢ Front Page   ➢ Business

> ➢ Portfolios   ➢ Entertainment

> ➢ Sports   ➢ Technology

This may be the easiest to set up for your preferences. There is a large registration form that includes: News (Business, Current Events, Health, Investing, Politics and Technology)

➢ Sports   ➢ Arts

➢ Entertainment   ➢ Lifestyles

➢ Music   ➢ Recreation

➢ Shopping   ➢ Technology

Technology includes Computing, Cyberculture, Multimedia and WWW Auditing. You simply mark each topic that interests you.

You can also enter the ticker symbols of your favorite stock quotes, mutual funds and commodities to have those quotes listed. There are also some icons such as My Internet (for Internet-related resources), My Contacts (has resources to help you find people and businesses) and New (this indicates a new web site within one of the categories or keywords you choose to monitor).

All the services mentioned above are free. You can also change any of your preferences at any time on all three.

You may have noticed that most of the sections are the same for all of these. You'll find most of the same stories at each one (as long as you kept your preferences the same, of course).

You should note that none of these will "stash and store" the information you may have missed by not checking in each day. It's virtually as if the newspaper is delivered each day but if you don't read it that day, someone throws it out and replaces it with a fresh one. As with most newspapers or other sources of news, you will definitely find one that you prefer over the others.

Hang On, We're Speed Browsing Now

Another way to help you manage the information available on the Internet are offline browsers. They've become quite popular and are designed to download and stash Web pages and files to your hard drive automatically for review later.

They work on customized preferences for each user, procuring only the information that fits your criteria. Another benefit to these products is the ability to review the information later when it's convenient for you, not dependent on an Internet connection.

One of the greatest advantages of these is the ability to prepare the information in an unattended mode so you can be doing other things such as eating or driving. By the time you're ready for your day, the information has already been collected and organized for you.

In choosing your offline browser, one of the factors to consider should be the ability to bundle your downloaded pages and files and to then export them to another computer (your laptop, perhaps, for viewing the information on the plane). Not all products offer this feature without having to mix software programs. Let's review a few of these products.

Individual Inc. Freeloader
www.freeloader.com

According to their web site, Freeloader delivers 20,000 news stories a day from nearly 600 information sources from around the world. Freeloader works on both a Windows and Macintosh platform, and is the only offline browser that is free!

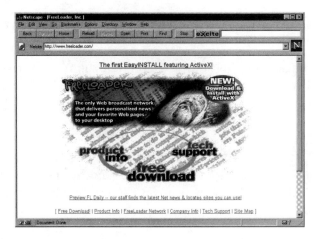

Their channels include:

> ➤ Arts & Style

> ➤ Computers & the Internet

> ➤ Family, Reference & Other

> ➤ Marketplace & Finance

> ➤ Music & Entertainment

> ➤ News, Weather & Politics

> ➤ Sports, Travel & Leisure

Some of the sources listed for the News, Weather & Politics channel are Congressional Quarterly, MSNBC, Netizen, News Page, Pathfinder, USA Today and 10-75.com.

Sources listed for the Marketplace & Finance are atOnce, Financial Resources Web Site, IBN: Internet Business Network and Quicken Financial Network.

The Computers & the Internet channel listed iWORLD, Jump City, NewsLinx, ZD Net and ZDNet Software Library as this sections sources. Freeloader is only offered via a download from the site.

To offer their advertisers some "dirt" on the user base, you will be asked to complete a form for some demographic information. Although this may not be the most advanced offline browser, for the price you can hardly pass the opportunity to try your hand at this technology.

DataViz Inc. Web Buddy
www.dataviz.com

"Meet your browser's best friend..." greets you at this site. It's available in Windows 95 and Macintosh platforms. A few of the options include the following:

- ➢ Page to Go
- ➢ Site to Go
- ➢ Schedule
- ➢ Convert
- ➢ Bookmark
- ➢ Organize

The Page- and Site to Go sections allow the user to easily save either a specific page or an entire site to your hard drive for review later. The Site to Go includes all links and graphics, so it appears to you just as it does on the Internet.

The Schedule option allows you to schedule a browse at a time that is convenient for you, such as early in the morning, so it does not interfere with your computer time. This also is nice as you can schedule the updates to run when the Internet is not so busy, saving additional time.

The Convert option available on Web Buddy is one of the few that allows you to use web pages and Internet graphics you have collected in your word processing or graphics programs.

In Bookmarks, you immediately organize your selected bookmarks into categories that you have selected or you can even create categories as you go. Use Web Buddy Central to archive and retrieve your information in an organized and easy way so that you don't have to search through all the files on your hard drive. Web Buddy is available in a Windows 95 or Macintosh trial version from their download area at the site. The complete package is available by diskette or by download right from the site.

Forefront Group WebWhacker
www.ffg.com

Recently named "Best of Test" for Offline Browsers by Internet World magazine, WebWacker is still trying to improve on its services. It's available in Windows 3.1, 95 and NT plus Macintosh platforms.

At this point we almost have to ask what does it not do. As is one of the charms of these products, you're able to set an overall updating schedule, but within this you can also specify particular update times for certain sites such as setting news sites to update at 6 am and 6 pm for round the clock news updates.

The toolbar that runs along the top of other applications allows for easy capture of URLs that you want to track once you have it displayed in a browser. These "whacked" sites can be exported into a compressed format for an easy transfer and can also include background sounds, Dynamic images, Shockwave objects, JPEG and GIF images and Java applets.

It does allow web sites and files that have been downloaded to be exported almost anywhere, from floppy discs to Zip drives. Its WebManager allows you to organize and categorize your sites for easy retrieval later. You're even able to search for text within the downloaded sites by keywords and Boolean terms.

A smart idea on their part is the ability to have WebWacker update itself through the Internet, delivering the latest version at the users command. The entire package is available on diskette or by download at the site.

Push 'em Back, Push 'em Back, Way Back

In an article in the May '97 issue of Internet World, Whit Andrews talks about the latest technology to sweep the Internet called *push technology* (also called *Webcasting*). "Push leverages the Internet's greatest fundamental asset – a universal network – to mitigate the unfortunate by-product of its own overwhelming success – access to too much information - by reversing the paradigm: It delivers proactively information we want or need; we no longer have to brave cyberspace to find it. More return for less effort."

At its best, push lets companies keep their employees abreast of important information. It lets companies keep their software current and it can bring Internet site visitors back often. Let's say that a banner with the company logo appears on your screen that says "Budget Reports due Tuesday."

By clicking on it, a form pops up on your browser. Once you have filled it out and click the Submit icon, it may check itself for errors and you're done. Whenever there are updates to your software, you (or the MIS person) would receive a message stating the update is available and ready to download without anyone having to track the upgrades.

General Motors uses push technology to make its training videos available to dealers. One company's product was developed specifically for Webmasters to entice visitors back to the site once they had already been there. By using various icons that spin and roll, visitors are informed of updates or new information to the site.

Maybe the best way to look at this is to consider your television. In reality, the programs that you watch are the result of a broadcaster's transmitting signal picked up by your tuner. In much the same way, push technology is sending out a signal that only those who have the proper tuner can intercept.

By setting your specifications, you limit the information that will be intercepted by your tuner so that you receive only the information you want, or perhaps the information that your company needs you to have.

With more people accessing the Internet and taking into account the number of web pages – 150 million as reported in Wired, March, 1997 – it's no wonder that new systems had to come into play. Even with a few great search engines, how can you possibly get through the maze of so much information?

That is much of the logic behind push technology. By delivering the news and information that is customized to your interests and specifications, you save much time and aggravation. "Do-it-yourself is great, but as in most aspects of life, people prefer ready-made. And when it comes to information, that means getting things from trusted sources" (Wired; March, 1997). Surprisingly, there are quite a few products to consider for this.

The following is a brief description of a few of these products.

PointCast Inc. PointCast Network
www.pointcast.com

Probably one of the first available using this technology, to date, this is also the only one that is free. Available in either the Windows 3.1 and Windows 95 platform, the Macintosh version is under development.

Your channel selection includes: News, Companies, Industries, Lifestyles, Sports and Weather. The News Channel includes Rueters national, international and business news headlines. With just a click on the headlines you want to review, you have access to the entire story. CNN news will be added soon.

The Companies Channel provides instant access to six weeks of stock prices, volume data and a scrolling stock ticker provided by Standard and Poor's Comstock, plus news from PR Newswire and Business Wire for companies that interest you.

The Industries Channel allows viewers to track news and information on more than 35 industries. These industries include:

- Advertising
- Computers/electronics
- Software
- Utilities

Current trading prices and volumes for nine major indices including NYSE, NASDAQ and Dow Jones Industrials are displayed. Your preferences can be changed at any time. This can be downloaded right from their site to your hard drive.

Intermind Communicator
www.intermind.com

Available in Macintosh, Windows 3.1, Windows 95 and Windows NT platforms with Unix in development.

Your channel topics include the following:

➢ Arts & Entertainment

➢ Business, Computers & Internet

➢ Health & Science

➢ News & Politics

➢ Retail & Shopping

➢ Society & Culture

➢ Sports, Travel & Leisure

The Business Channel includes such sources as:

> ➢ Bizhead Alert!   ➢ Business Case Web Site
>
> ➢ EDGAR Online   ➢ Internet Database Marketing

The News & Politics Channel lists CBS News Up to the Minute, GOP News Wire, Group Web eJournal, Politics Online and WORLD Netday News as sources. Once the agents have encountered a change in one of the sites you are following, it will either trigger an alert or deliver the new content according to your specifications.

Wayfarer INCISA
www.wayfarer

ZD Internet Magazine was recently named INCISA "Best Choice" for Push Technology. It's currently available on Windows 3.1, Windows 95 and Windows NT platform and a Macintosh version is being developed.

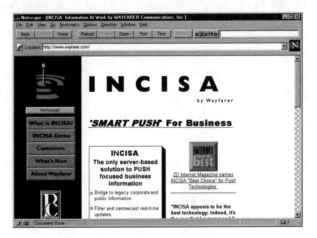

While some of the other products rely on content from the Internet, INCISA is designed more for the intranets of companies to maximize the use of "push" technology to get relevant business information to their employees desktops.

With a format that is easy to work from, you can use this for messages from the president, special event reminders and headlines of relevant business news. You can direct information to everyone, specific groups or individuals. Energy, finance, government, health care and high technology are some of key segments that INCISA covers. PC Quote, Reuters Online News Service and PR Newswire were the original sources for outside news and information.

However, they recently added three information distributors – Infoseek, Infonautics and Comtex – along with CNET, PC World, USA Today and Warfield Media Company.

In what is probably some of the biggest news for Wayfarer, Netscape will use Wayfarer's Push technology to support its new Netcaster.

One Moment Please, Let Me Check My Database

Another place to find information for your research are the fee-based or subscription database services. As most anyone will agree, these are probably the most reliable sources of information, as it has all been verified.

There are quite a few of these services available, with some specific to certain areas of industry or type of information. Sometimes compared to the old "clipping services," they basically have done the work for you. You just need to contact them, tell them what information you are looking for and they will find it for you.

The main appeal is that these services have access to information that is almost impossible for the mere mortal to obtain (even with our crafty ways!). However you will note that I said *fee-based* or *subscription*. The following are some of the most well-known and often referred to for business and competitive information.

Lexis-Nexis
www.lexis-nexis.com

This is the premier online information service. They claim to have over one billion documents online. It started in 1973 with LEXIS, the first full-text legal information service. NEXIS was added in 1979 as the business information partner. Today, LEXIS-NEXIS (L-N) has more than 13,500 sources (8700 newsletters and 4800 legal).

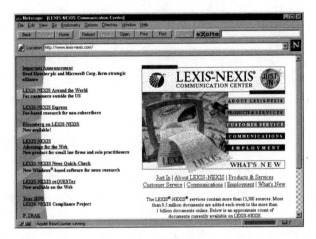

L-N, based in Dayton, Ohio, has 788,000 active users in over 60 countries. The databases (numbering over 7300) can be searched 3 ways:

> FREESTYLE (TM)

> Boolean

> Easy Search (TM)

The LEXIS service includes archives of federal and state case law, updated statutes for all 50 states, state and federal regulations and public records from some US states. The service has 41 specialized libraries that cover all major fields of practice, including banking, energy, environmental, international and tax.

Of the over 8700 sources for the NEXIS service, 3700 of those provide the entire publication online. The service includes regional, national and international newspapers, magazines, newswires, trade journals and business publications.

It also contains both national and regional television broadcast transcripts, plus CNN and National Public Radio news and features. The NEXIS service also offers brokerage house and industry analyst reports business information from Dunn & Bradstreet public records such as corporate filings and property records and tax information.

The topics libraries include business and finance, computers and communications, energy, entertainment and environment. LEXIS-NEXIS does feature a few customized services that cater to those who have a very specific search in mind.

NewsNet
www.newsnet.com

With a slogan like "Working Knowledge," you just know you're going to like them! Since 1982 NewsNet has been a providing online business information to busy executives. Their resources include 1000 newsletters, magazines and newspapers and over 30 worldwide newswires.

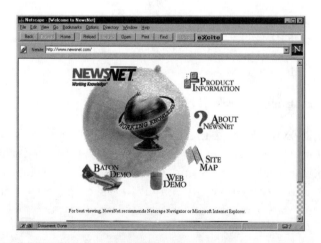

At last count, there were 51 categories of resources from Advertising and Marketing to Xinhua. Among the categories are a few very valuable resources such as Dunn & Bradstreet Information Services' Online Service, PR NewsWire and Standard & Poor's. You can access the information you are looking for a few different ways:

> ➤ Browse headlines of current periodicals and newswires

> ➤ Search using Boolean keyword logic or plain English phrases

> ➤ Use their NewsFlash personal clipping agent.

NewsFlash monitors the NewsNet database 24 hours a day for the articles on the specific topics that the user has identified as part of their criteria.

As part of the service, you receive the NewsNet Action Letter and a semi-monthly update that tells of title changes has a NewsNet FAQs column and small articles to assist you in your research. One the best finds here is the customer service.

When contacted regarding some information, they were very helpful and followed up more than once to be sure that the questions had been answered and that we had the information we needed.

Profound
www.profound.com

Claiming to have over 1 million pages of information, you know that you have to at least check this out! With one single search, you are able access all of their databases, which include IAC ASAP IAC Industry Express and IAC Newsletter databases.

The ASAP contains full-text business journals and current company data and is composed of four specialty databases:

- ➤ Trade & Industry

- ➤ Magazines

- ➤ Computer

- ➤ Health & Wellness

The Industry Express is a combination of a rolling 30-day period of content from leading trade and business publications. It offers information on such industry segments as biotechnology, computers, electronics, health care, telecommunications and drugs & pharmaceuticals. The Newsletter section contains more than 600 full-text newsletters from all over the world.

One of the best features is its acceptability right up front. As it's platform independent, it will work on your system if you have Mac, PC, OS/2 or Unix workstations and an Internet browser such as Netscape's Navigator or Microsoft's Explorer. Simply type in the Internet address, sign in, and you're ready to go. Customer service for this was very good, too. We were contacted more than once to be sure that our questions had been answered and that we had all the information we needed.

The Case
Studies

Part 4

11

Introducing The Case Studies

Introducing The Case Studies

We outlined the Internet in Part 1, Competitive Intelligence in Part 2 and used them together in Part 3. Now in Part 4 well talk about examples of applied competitive intelligence.

The four case studies cover service, manufacturing, retail and a large public corporation. The idea of these is just to take basic information from the company, assess what they are looking for and then suggest a few options for them to look into.

The object is to get the first three companies started on the competitive intelligence track. Not only will they have the resources to get the specific information that they need, but also the general industry information that they should be monitoring on an continuing basis. The last study explains some of the resources from which to gather important information on larger, publicly-held companies.

Although some of this information or some of the resources may seem repetitive, it takes a lot of different information—meaningfully assembled—to form a clear and accurate representation of the market and competitors.

12

A Food Service Consultant In West Michigan

A Food Service Consultant In West Michigan

Information provided by company:

Competitors: Annapolis, MD   SIC Codes: Unknown

Englewood, CO

New York, NY   Markets: National - Health Care

Situation: This company just wants to find as much information on their competitors as possible. As all of the companies involved are quite small, there seems to be very little information available about any of them.

First, we want to verify the competitors' addresses. It's important to find the most specific mailing address, as many companies near big cities are frequently listed as being in that city. For example, some directories list the Englewood, CO, company as being in Denver, the nearest major city. InfoSpace, at www.infospace.com, is quite helpful for finding correct addresses. Having the right address will save considerable time when searching databases or specifying reports.

Next we'll continue the search for information in local newspapers. Using Editor & Publisher (www.mediainfo.com/ephome/npaper/nphtm/online.htm), News Source (www.newo.com/news) and the Newspaper Association of America (www.naa.org/hot/index.html), the *Capital* (Annapolis), *Denver Post & Rocky Mountain News* (Denver/Englewood), and *New York Times* (New York) were identified as good sources of local news.

Typically, the CI agent should be scanning these newspapers for information about new contracts, hirings, layoffs, job postings, possible tax liens, local court cases and maybe even features on the competitors. Unless the researcher is checking the on-line papers each day, he/she needs to consider subscribing to these newspapers to be sure that they receive all of the information.

Due to the general and business environment in New York, the *NYTimes* may not have much information on the competing company. In this case, you may want to look into smaller, maybe borough-specific papers that will pay more attention to local businesses.

Food Service Consultants Society International (FCSI) (ww2.fcsi.org/fcsi), Design Build Institute of America (DBIA) (www.dbia.org), The National Society of Healthcare Food Service Management (HFM) (www.hfm.org/htm) and American Society for Hospital Food Service Administration (ASHFSA) are associations that should be explored.

The FCSI site has a bulletin board where members (they are not kidding here; you cannot even access it for topics without being a member!) can gather important information. The FCSI also offers a quarterly publication, *The Consultant*, which covers the issues and news important to the industry. The HFM site offers News & Information, Contacts and "The Web," a section that has Interesting Food & Healthcare Sites on the Web and Links to Associate Member Web sites.

They also have a section just for Networking Opportunities. Remember that associations are one place to find the industry experts, and *those* are the folks with whom this company wants to network.

It should be noted here that these organizations had been searched for through most of the search engines, only to find nothing. In a bold move, the initials were entered as the URL (i.e.: *www.fcsi.org*) and the site was found immediately. Don't be afraid of this technology, people; it is our friend!

Somewhat like local newspapers, trade publications also list new hires and new contracts, along with the possible company spotlight. However, almost always, the information that is covered in trade publications is information that the company wants to be covered (often with press releases, etc.).

Restaurant & Institutions (www.rimag.com) is one of the publications that pertains to this specific segment of the industry. Others to look into include *Food Service Director* and *Food Management*. Publications such as these do provide research and reports on the general industry, tracking the economic indicators that pertain to the industry. Also, the editors of these trade magazines are the people that this company wants to get to know, since they are some of the first people in an industry to know about most anything, from new product developments to mergers and buy-outs.

Running the terms "Food Service Consultant" through various search engines created a little confusion; there seemed to be too many terms. Linking terms didn't always help, either. However, once the search term was revised to "Architects," more progress was made. This company had said that they sometimes worked for architects as subcontractors. Almost all of the sites that pertained to architects had sections that included "Other Professional Services," "Consultants," "Food Service" and so on.

Inter Trade (www.itrade.net), for the Food Industry Online, turned out to be an interesting find, too. It offers information areas of a Company Directory, Catalogs Online, News & Classified, Hot New Products and About Inter Trade.

The options at the News & Classified section from which you can choose are the following:

- Employment Wanted

- Employment Offered

- Special Promotions

- Used & Surplus Equipment

- Industry News

Don't forget to search those job postings; there may be something in there that is worth looking into a little more.

The Company Directory included Consulting and Design sections where the 3 competitors were listed, but oddly enough, this company was not. All three were listed under Consulting: Food Facility and Operations, plus Design: Facility Design and only the Colorado-based competitor was listed under Interior Design.

AEC (Architecture, Engineering, and Building Construction) Info Center (www.aecinfo.com) was also a very good find. It included such areas as the Building Product Library, Support Services and Software & Hardware. It also included SpecCenter, Feature Article, Government & Authorities and Interactive Forums. The forums included Product Discussions and Professional, which are set up just like newsgroups with a posting to be responded to. There were 16 product categories to choose from, making it quite specific to an area of interest. Within the

Architecture area, there was a Consulting area titled "Food Service." However, none of the competitors nor this company were listed. This would be a good place to enter the forums and see what is going on, along with what is being said about the competitors.

Another interesting aspect of this industry is it's relationship to the government. As many of the healthcare facilities are government related (military, etc.), there are a few sources that should be visited at least once in a while.

The SSA Procurement Opportunities (www.ssa.gov/oag/acq/toc.htm) offers up projects that are put out for bids by private contractors. As these projects are listed under Categories, this company would only have to check those areas to see what projects were up for bids.

These resources listed are by no means the only places to look for information on the competitors and the industry. While this company is looking for particular information, regarding only 3 competitors, they also need to start building a base of general industry information.

With new competitors entering and old ones leaving, it's important to know the overall picture. Of course, most of the resources already reviewed will also assist in building their base of information as has been indicated along the way. However, another source of information on specific industries includes the Occupational Outlook Handbook section available on the Bureau of Labor Statistics site, stats.bls.gov.oco/ocos038.htm.

These reports include Nature of the Work background, Working Conditions, Employment, Training, Job Outlook, Earnings, Related Occupations and Sources of Additional Information. In looking under Architects, this report mentioned the need for schools and health care facilities due to changing demographics; nice information to know in the field.

It also mentioned that the employment growth for this field is expected to increase about as fast as the average for all occupations.

This is also when the company should be reviewing the various news sources, such as Business Wire, CNN Interactive, News Page, PR Newswire and Reuters. Even though the news will only cover the larger companies—generally—it is still a good idea for them to know what is going in the industry as a whole. Major developments will probably be reported in a timelier manner through these daily sources than by the monthly industry trade publications!

Another source to consider are the architects with who they sometimes partner on projects. As those architects must surely work with the competitors, too, they could be a great source of information. As in building relationships with the editors and key industry figures, these would be good contacts.

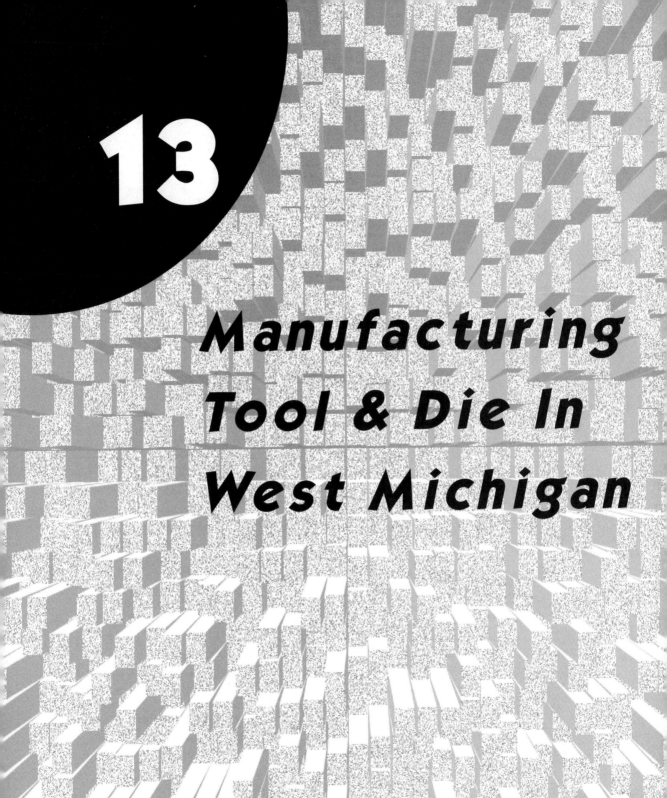

13

Manufacturing Tool & Die In West Michigan

Manufacturing Tool & Die In West Michigan

Information provided by company:

Competitors: Chicago, IL   SIC Group: 3544

Grand Rapids, MI

Saginaw, MI   Markets: Mid-West

Situation: This company would like to know how their competitors are marketing themselves in an effort to better position themselves in this very competitive market place. They have reported that the market place for their manufacturing process is very limited, and so competition is very fierce.

First, as with Case A (and always), the addresses for the competitors should be verified. Some listings will give the most specific city name, which you may need for certain agencies when requesting information. The general directories are not always very dependable for business information, so you may need to try industry-specific sites for listings, too. InfoSpace (www.infospace.com), Industry Net (www.industry.net) and Thomas Register (www.thomasregister.com) are useful in getting the actual addresses of these competitors.

Industry-specific sites, such as the two listed above—Industry Net and Thomas Register—are also a good place to look up the competitors to see what their listings consist of, or if they are listed at all. In putting a search out for the product categories of this company, are the competitors coming up too? If not, they will have to find out how the competitors are classifying their products.

The next step would be to look up the local newspapers and/or business journals in the above areas. The *Chicago Sun-Times,* the *Chicago Tribune*, the *Grand Rapids Press* and the *Saginaw News* were found by searching Editor & Publisher's Online Newspapers (www.mediainfo.com/ephome/npaper/nphtm/online.htm) and the Newspaper Association of America's Hotlinks (www.naa.org/hot/index.html).

Although the company can access the news right from these web sites (and it is more timely) they should consider a regular subscription to be sure that they get every day's news from each source. In these local newspapers, they will want to be on the look out for items that may include hirings, layoffs, court cases, tax liens or maybe even an interview or article spotlighting the competitor(s).

In staying with the traditional print media, *Intelligent Manufacturing* magazine and *Engineering & Technology Resources* may be publications to check out for any advertising the competitors may be running. While these will also tend to carry mainly approved PR items, they may be lucky and find interviews or articles that feature the competitor(s).

These industry-specific publications are also good for general industry information such as trends and economic studies. Again, they should begin to cultivate relationships with the editors; it is never to soon to start introducing themselves to these key individuals.

Using Publicly Accessible Mailing Lists (www.neosoft.com/internet/paml) and Deja News (www.dejanews.com), there was not much luck to be had looking for "Tool & Die" or even "Manufacturing."

However, there were *several* job postings at both sources—bingo! This is yet another source to see if their competitors are hiring and for what positions/skills they are looking (obviously a purchasing clerk position would not be as interesting as an engineer with a background in a different industry). Industry Net (www.industry.net) did prove to be a great find for Business & Industry Internet Newsgroups.

Some of newsgroups to consider looking into would be alt.business.industrial, alt.manufacturing.misc, comp.robotics.misc, misc.jobs and sci.engr.manufacturing. The CI agent may even want to start a news group that focuses on some specific manufacturing process in which they specialize.

If it is presented under their name from the beginning, they may get competitors' customers looking for answers that the competitor is not addressing, thus giving this company an idea of one—or several—quality or manufacturing advantages.

One area that should not be over-looked, even if it does not necessarily pertain to the Internet, is the sales force. These people usually know a lot of what is going on and what is being said about the company as well as the competitors.

However, they do need to be "officially" notified by the main office as to what information they should *really* be paying attention to. In this case, any information about the competitors' machinery, tooling processes or even pricing strategy needs to be immediately fed back to a single contact.

Even if this company thinks they know the machinery that their competitors are using, it is highly advisable that they obtain the Uniform Commercial Code reports on these competitors.

As this should list all of the on-premise assets they will have a much better idea of what the competitors are using in relation to their own machines.

The Secretary of State should have those records on file, so the Michigan and Illinois branches need to be contacted at www.sos.state.mi.us and www.sos.state.il.us respectively for the immediate competitors listed.

In looking for associations that this company may want to be more involved in, a few to consider would be The Association of Manufacturing Technology, The National Tooling and Machining Association, The Tooling and Manufacturing Association and the Society of Manufacturing Engineers (www.sme.org).

While not all of these have Web sites, the contact information is available and they can pursue those associations by other means. Remember, the Internet is not intended to replace any venue already in use. The SME site states that "SME is an international professional society dedicated to serving its members and the manufacturing community through the advancement of professionalism, knowledge, and learning."

Membership includes technology-specific public forums offered on SME ON-LINE and the Manufacturing Network, SME's electronic bulletin board, plus published trade publications, quarterly technical publications and technical reports. Not only will the company get additional insight on the competitors, but they can also find the "key contacts" such as analysts with who they should be developing relations.

Another part of the SME site was the CoNDUIT project. This project is aimed at improving workforce training delivery and the transfer of technology through a network that links community colleges to manufacturing expertise in an effort to get manufacturing education to small and mid-sized businesses. Well, this seems like a good place to start to see if the competitors are involved with any of the community colleges.

While pursuing the higher educational facilities, College Net (www.collegenet.com) turned out to be a good place to locate colleges and universities. There were a total of 55 colleges & university links listed for Michigan and 74 for Illinois.

Those listed for Michigan included GMI Engineering & Management/ Ann Arbor and Lawrence Technology/Southfield. The Illinois listings included DeVry Institute of Technology/Addison & Chicago and Illinois Institute of Technology/Chicago. If they do not know which institutions offer the programs that may be of interest to their industry, they can check out the home pages for the institutions that should be contacted to see if the competitors are involved in any projects with these places.

While this company is looking for specific information as it relates to their competitors, they should also be getting sources together for an overall check on the industry. As was mentioned earlier, Competitive Intelligence should be an ongoing activity that monitors the general environment—in this case manufacturing, and specifically tool and die.

If this company only watched the immediate competitors, they might miss out on some far-reaching general industry news or developments and might even miss the intentions of some company that *will* become a competitor. As with Case Study A, the resources already suggested will provide a great deal of information and the contacts necessary to establish the overall industry picture. However, this company needs to keep in mind that these resources are only a *few* of the available out there; explore!

They should never assume that they have "enough" or "all" of the information, as that would be next to impossible (given the size of the Internet). They also need to be looking for news sources that cover the industry and manufacturing news along with the trade publications in which they were looking for competitor information. The associations are also useful for up-to-date information on industries and developments related to the industry. Government sites, such as the

Bureau of Labor Statistics (stats.bls.gov/blshome.htm), provide such reports as the Occupational Outlook Handbook that details specific occupations—Tool & Die Makers, for one—that include Nature of the Work, Employment and Job Outlook, plus some resources related to the industry.

The Census Bureau (www.census.gov) has current industry reports that include Productivity Indexes, etc. By looking at Business Wire, News Page, News Source, PR Newswire and Reuters—just to name a few—they can get an idea of what sources cover their industry best, along with the industries that affect their own. There are a lot of other sources listed within this book, along with several others on the Net, that can be very useful; they, along with all the other companies, just have to be willing to put some time into it.

14

Retail Hardware Store

Retail Hardware Store

Markets: Local

Situation: For this case, there is no existing company or business. Keeping in mind the earlier example of the Hardware Store, this shall be the follow through on that example.

There has been no location to setup this business, yet. The first thing to do was find some sites that offered some information on this industry. In having a go at the search engines, "hardware" was difficult as a lot of computer hardware sites were included in the results. "Hardware industry" did work much better, although there were still plenty of computer-related sites. "Tools" resulted in much the same type of results as "hardware" as, again, the computer industry uses that term, too!

A couple of the results were quite useful and some turned out to be associations. The first, the National Retail Hardware Association (www.nrha.org), had a lot of very helpful information available. Not only is there quite a bit of sales information, the site also offers an Industry Overview for the Retail Hardware/Home Improvement Market and for Hardlines Distribution.

In keeping with the retail idea, they offer up a report that includes a general introduction along with a brief description of the 4 main retail types: Hardware Stores, Home Centers, Warehouse Home Centers and the Consumer-Oriented Lumberyards, plus a brief about the Role of Retail Chains.

There are also some Market Research reports available for a fee that include "Benchmarks for Success," "Defining Customer Satisfaction for the Do-It-Yourself Customer," and the "1995 Cost of Doing Business." A grand bonus to membership at the NRHA is a monthly publication, *Do-It-Yourself Retailing,* which covers management, marketing and merchandising information.

Another association site, the American Hardware Manufacturing Association (www.ahma.org), had a lot of useful information, too. Their mission, as stated on the home page, is "to be the world's leading resource on and about the U.S. manufacturing segment of the worldwide consumer hardware/home improvement marketplace." This site offers New Products Online (browse by manufacturer or 1 of 12 product listings that include Hand Tools, Power Tools and Hardware; or simply enter keywords) plus Industry News, an Industry Calendar, library and Convention & Conferences.

Hardware World (www.hardwareworld.com) was also found in the quest for information on Hardware Stores. This site claims to have "the Internet's Largest Assortment of Hardware and Home Improvement Sites." It is broken down into 6 sections: New, Products, Retailers, Distributors, Other (Tim Allen links can be found here, too!) and Web stuff. This would be a good place to check out once you know who your competitors are; are they listed, too?

In looking at some other resources for industry information, the Occupational Outlook Handbook—under Retail Sales Workers— reported that the 1994 median weekly earnings for Hardware & Building Supplies was $ 333. The report also said that the job outlook, or employment rate, was growing faster than the average. First, this means that the average worker was making $ 8.33 an hour if they were working a 40-hour work week. It also means that there was an employment increase to be expected for this segment.

If it did not matter where the store was to be—that there was absolute freedom in the decision—then you should look into some sources that would report on the factors that go into a successful retail store, such as population growth, economic status and so on. As it is a large site, the US Business Advisor (www.business.gov) would be a good place to spend some time.

Not only can you get the population reports, from the Census Bureau (www.census.gov), but also some of the economic information at the Bureau of Labor Statistics (stats.bls.gov/blshome.html) that includes the Consumer Price Indexes and Prices & Living Conditions reports. The Business Advisor site also had sections that include "Start a Business," "Finance a Business" and even "Get a Service Corps of Retired Executives Counseling Appointment."

As a different approach, you may want to try publications such as *Business Week* and *Inc* that put out articles on the "Best Places to Live in the USA" or some such title. These may have very interesting data or criteria you had not yet thought of that could help you decide on a certain geographic location for your store.

Now it would be advisable to do some market research. You should scout the mailing lists and newsgroups for hardware discussions. Although none could be found on either Deja News or the Neosoft's Listserv list, you still need to keep trying.

This is a good way to learn what people are looking for in a hardware store and what is wrong with the way they are operating now. What can be done better? This does not necessarily have to be done before you choose the location, but it may help to know what the preference is in your exact area.

Once you have secured your location, you will want to get all of the local information you can on your competitors. Of course, the local newspapers and business journals will be the most help. Another source of information is to simply go shopping! Visit the competitors and see what their pricing strategy is and what their after-sales policies and terms are.

To be even more specific, you may want to look into some government filings to see what their overhead is: What is everyone paying in rent and hired help? You may want to contact some of the government offices, or better yet, get back in touch with the US Business Advisor site.

By asking exactly what information you need, it is more than likely that they can tell you *if* it is of public record and if so, what agency from which to request it. The more that you know about them, the fewer surprises there will be down the road.

As the market is local and the competitors are few (that is why you choose the location you did!), some of other resources don't work quite as well. It might be a consideration to look into some sites that offer assistance and information for small businesses (in addition to the Business Advisor) such as the SmallbizNet at Resource Connection (edgeonline.com/main/resourcepage/).

There are many sites that cater to the small business sector, and you should be able to find them listed under most business sources.

Another strategy may be to monitor any new products that enter the market. While it may be more costly to jump on such items, it may pay off in the end with loyalty.

To keep up on the latest products, trade shows would certainly be a good place to see a lot of stuff in a small amount of time. Both the NRHA and AHMA offered plenty of information on the national and regional shows.

Get industry information. Visit association sites. Check out Hardware World and the Occupational Outlook Handbook to learn about potential employment increases. Research demographics and the business climate of areas where you may open the store.

Use market research obtained through usenet and listserv to keep yourself on the leading edge of developing issues. Most importantly, learn about competitors with the examples above. Each of these is an important element of the competitive intelligence assembled for this project.

15

A Consumer Beverage Corporation

A Consumer Beverage Corporation

Markets: International

As all of the case studies have been privately-held companies, in smaller industries, it is the intention of this case to briefly show how much additional information is available for publicly-held companies. In using the company name only as the query term with some of the search engines, there were between 42,000 and 60,000 returns listed. Surprisingly, the company home page was *not* within even the first 40 returns! Everything from someone's own homepage for the company to QVC's listing of it's merchandise and the "official" story of how the company began (**not** at the home page) were included in the initial returns.

Sites such as NASDAQ (www.nasdaq.com) and many others that carry this specific information are available for immediate stock quotes, usually along with articles that mention the company. This is the interesting part of publicly-held companies: you can actually track your competitor (assuming that they are also publicly-held) on a *daily* basis. With so much market information and news, CI is a whole different ball game!

Being international in scope, and considering it size, it is no wonder that the company always seems to be in the news. There are acquisitions, even court cases of some sort all over the world; there are spokes-people to sign and let go; and there is still the business of beverages and how to do it better than the competitor(s). This is the type of company that Business Wire, PR Newswire and Reuters do justice to.

Many resources are available for obtaining information on a publicly-held company's finances and stocks. A search of EDGAR (www.sec.gov/edgarhp.htm) by a company's name will get you the Central Index Key, Current Events Analysis (including 10-K annual, 10-K quarterly, Shareholders Meetings Reports and Proxies) plus the Schedule 13D Ownership Report and even a method to find Executive Compensation's using the DEF 14A filing. Sites such as Corporate Financials Online (www.cfo.com) offer the latest quarterly reports for many of the publicly-held companies.

At Wall Street Research Net (www.wsrn.com) it is possible to research a publicly-held company. Entering the query into the search returned an incredible amount of information. The Company Links section included the Home Page and SEC Filings. The News Center included company news. The Charts & Graphs section offered Current Quotes (by NASDAQ) and a NASDAQ Graph for the past 6 months. The Research, Reports and Summaries included earnings estimates and industry comparisons. I ask you, can it get any easier than this? Yes, it probably can, but this is still much easier than looking for information on the private sector.

To look into the industry a bit more, the National Soft Drink Association (www.nsda.org/home.html) seems to have it all. There are 5 listings available here that include a report on the "Economic Impact of the Industry," Industry Web Links, Market Research, Franchise Companies and their Brands, and Soft Drink Suppliers.

The Products section lists 8 reports that include "Growing Up Together...," "The History of America and Soft Drinks...," and "Your Favorite Soft Drink." There is a Recycling section along with Issues and Events. Not only is it somewhat entertaining to visit, but there is a lot of useful information there as well!

Another site to check out was Bev Net (www.thebevnet.com) where they suggest that you "Drink Yourself Silly." While not quite as comprehensive at the NSDA site, this did have sections for Reviews (yes, beverage reviews), Industry (news & classifieds, also known as the Marketplace), Features, Bev Board (a bulletin board for the industry), Business information and Links.

Beverage Digest (www.beverage-digest.com) is a newsletter and information source that includes information from the latest issue, conference information, the Top 10 Rankings (and this is done on a chart with many different indicators included), information to order the *Beverage Digest Fact Book,* and links to numerous beverage sites. Again, as it should not matter how large your corporation is, a good way to see what is going in the industry is to check out the Bev Board.

What is being said about your corporation? About the competitor? Are there new products in the works by anyone other than the "usual" companies? Also, someone should be watching the classifieds; after all, what better place to find someone for your industry than at a site such as this?!

The Internet has many resources for gathering intelligence about most companies, but especially publicly-held companies. Whether you need stocks, news, reports of shareholders meetings or information on the market, the 'Net should be your first stop for preliminary research.

Appendix

Part 5

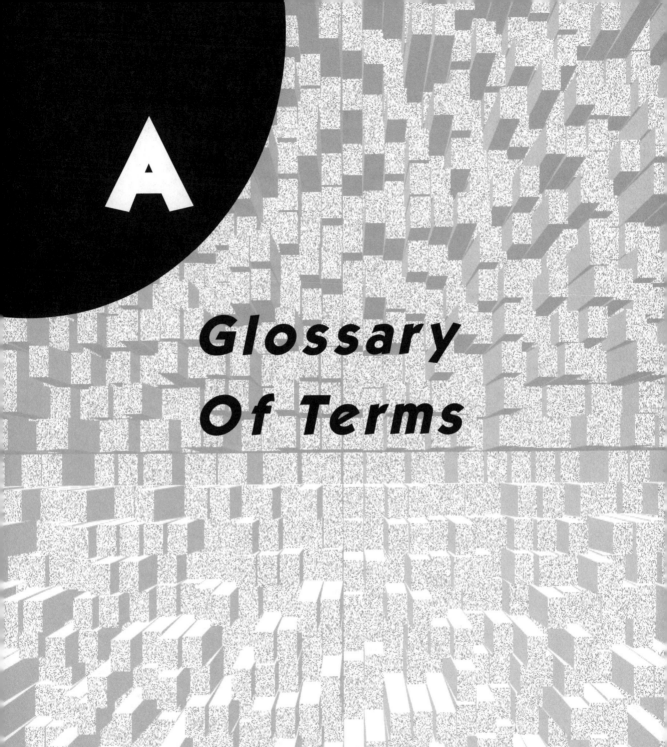

A

Glossary Of Terms

Glossary Of Terms

Administrator

Manages a network or partial areas of a network, possessing rights that go beyond the rights of the normal user (e.g., password management).

API

(Acronym for Application Programming Interface) Collection and specification of data formats, software interrupts etc., which can be used by applications to connect with mainframes, network programs, etc.

ASCII

Text that is not formatted with HTML (see HTML). You'll also see ASCII text called *plain text* or *text documents*.

Bookmark

A feature on most web browsers that let you store the addresses of web pages that you visit frequently. By using bookmarks you don't have to remember or retype your favorite web site addresses. A bookmark is also called a "hotlist."

Browser

Software program used to read and download HTML documents and Web file and pages.

Client

A client uses the services of a server, in other words, a system that is connected to a network and makes use of its (shared) resources.

Client-server network (Client-Server Architecture)

A network architecture with resources concentrated on one or more powerful server computers that can be used by connected client systems (workstations).

Domain

A local grouping of several servers and resources in Windows NT. A single entity administers the domain.

Downloading

The act of moving pictures, programs, files, etc. *from* a web site or online service *to* your computer. Downloading is the opposite of uploading.

E-mail

Abbreviation for electronic mail. A method of communicating with other users over the Internet. Also refers to the messages themselves that are sent on a network using a computer.

Emoticons

Text symbols representing emotions that are used in E-mail or chat rooms. Most emoticons are read sideways, so ":)" represents being happy and ":(" represents being sad.

External viewer

See Helper application

FAQ

(Acronym for Frequently Asked Questions) A text file that lists and answers commonly asked questions on a particular topic. FAQ files are important sources of discovering information about the Internet.

FTP

(Acronym for File Transfer Protocol) An easy method of transferring files between computers on the Internet.

Helper application (Helper apps)

Programs that you can link to different file types and commands. These programs launch automatically when you access a linked file through a browser.

Hits

The number of times a specific file is accessed at a Web site.

Home page

The document that is first displayed when you start up a web browser. This is the main page of a Web site.

HTML

(Acronym for Hypertext Markup Language) The standard programming language used to create Web pages. These codes tell a browser how to display the text, hyperlinks, graphics and attached media of the document. HTML documents are essentially text documents with embedded tags that contain the codes for formatting, graphics, etc. Also called hypertext.

HTTP

(Acronym for HyperText Transfer Protocol) A protocol used to transmit and link Web pages. It's the standard language used by Web browsers and servers to communicate with each other.

Hyperlink

A reference in an HTML document (word, picture or button) that when clicked, takes you to another Web page or another part of the current page. Same as link.

Hypermedia

Incorporating nontext media in one document using hyperlinks.

Internet

An interconnected group of worldwide computer networks using standard computer formats to exchange information and other data.

Internet Service Provider (ISP)

Companies that provide connections, for a monthly or hourly fee, to the Internet. ISPs provide only a direct Internet connection. They do not provide instructions or interest catalogs to help you navigate through the Internet.

Java

Programming language for embedding small applications called Java applets into Web pages. Java allows Web developers to write programs that will run on any computer with a Java-capable browser (i.e., Netscape or Internet Explorer).

Java applets

Small programs written in Java that are sent over the Internet and normally run inside a Web browser window. Most Java applets are currently used for minor functions like running simple animations.

Kbps

(Acronym for kilobits per second) Refers to the speed at which data is transferred over a line. One kilobit equals 1000 bits so a 28.8Kbps modem transfers data at a rate of 28,800 bits per second.

Maintain

To regularly update a WWW site.

Multimedia

Combining and using several types of media, including graphics, audio and video, into one resource or program file. A powerful means of communicating information.

NDIS

(Acronym for Network Driver Interface Specification) Specifies the interaction between a transport utility and a device driver. Originally defined by Microsoft, NDIS is now accepted on the market.

Page

One HTML-based document that you can view using a browser (also called a Web page).

PDF

(Acronym for Portable Document Format) Adobe Systems created PDF to be the dominant format for transferring documents between incompatible computers. This lets users of PDF to print out these documents. PDF files can be accessed by using Adobe's Acrobat reader or the Amber plug-in.

PERL

(Acronym for Practical Extraction and Report Language) PERL is used by Web developers to create dynamic pages and scripts for processing forms.

Protocol

Specification of rules and procedures governing the transfer of information with data connections on networks. Unfortunately, there is still no uniform standard, thus different protocols exist alongside one another and must take each other into account.

Router

Hardware component responsible for connecting two network subsystems using the shortest route available.

Server

Powerful computer or program that concentrates resources (files, date, applications, etc.) on a network and makes them available to clients. A network can have more than one server.

Supervisor

The supervisor is responsible for security on the network and makes sure that the network functions smoothly. The supervisor enjoys all the rights on the network. Supervisors can assign and restrict rights on the network.

TCP/IP

(Acronym for Transmission Control Protocol/Internet Protocol) Standard protocol for wide area networks (WAN).

Terminal

Combination of monitor and keyboard.

UART

(Acronym for Universal Asynchronous Receiver/Transmitter) Manages the data sent from your communications software to the modem. The UART is located on the motherboard. Internal modems include the UART as part of its hardware.

Uploading

The act of moving pictures, programs, files, etc. *to* a web site or online service *from* your computer. Uploading is the opposite of downloading.

URL

(Acronym for Uniform Resource Locator) Addressing system used in the WWW that can reference any type of file on the Internet. A Web browser can locate that file because this address is unique to each page. A typical Web URL looks like this:

http://www.pcnovice.com.

User

A user can be assigned rights and be administered in an account, or user account. The user logs on to the network by means of a password.

Web

Abbreviation for World Wide Web (see World Wide Web)

Web page

Refers to one document on the Web. A web page can include a combination of text, pictures, video and sound.

Web site

A collection of web pages maintained by a business, institution, individual, organization, etc.

Webmaster

A person responsible for administering a WWW site.

World Wide Web (WWW)

A network of hypertext documents on the Internet that can be navigated with a browser and are connected through hyperlinks.

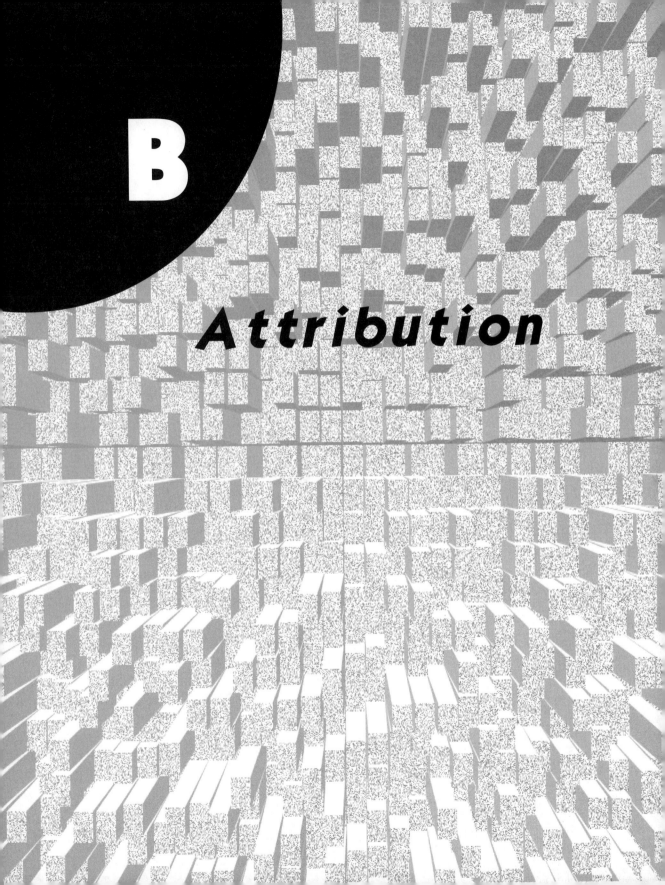

B

Attribution

Attribution

Expert Interviews

Lewis, Bryan; VP, Fusionary Media, Grand Rapids, Michigan. August 13, 1996; August 18, 1996; April 2, 1997; April 9, 1997.

Ubaldo, Joe; Macintosh Systems Design & Support, Mac | Vision, Grand Rapids, Michigan. March 26, 1997.

Web Sites

Bragg, Fawn, "What is a listserv?" cyberschool.4j.lane.edu/People/Fac...Bragg/APEng1/Help/Listservs/Listserv.html. April 24, 1997.

"WWW Hot Topic: Internet 25th Anniversary" www.amdahl.com/internet/events/inet25.html. Amdahl Corporation, July 18, 1996.

"The Name. Some History" sual05.cern.ch/CERN.html. CERN, April 8, 1997.

Small Business Services. www.dnb.com/dbis/sbs/hsbs.htm. Dun & Bradstreet, March 22, 1997.

Zakon, Robert H'obbes', "Hobbes' Internet Timeline v2.1" www.handshake.de/infobase/netze/internet/hit.htm, The MITRE Corporation, April 8, 1997.

"A Brief History of theNSFNET Program" www.mr.net/resources/nsfnetprogram.html, MRNet, May 15, 1997.

Graef, Jean L., "Using the Internet for Competitive Intelligence" www.montoague.com/scip/sio.html, Montague Institute, July 20, 1996.

Treese, Win, "The Internet Index" www.openmarket.com/intindex/96-12.htm. OpenMarket, April 2, 1997.

Treese, Win, "The Internet Index" www.openmarket.com/intindex/97-04.htm. OpenMarket, May 13, 1997.

"The Internet" www.ipxnet.com/home/yankee/college/internet.htm. The Research Paper Home Page, May 14,1997.

"35 Free Facts for Competitive Intelligence Professionals" www.trainer.com/pub/busintel/freefacts.html. Washington Researchers Ltd., April 20, 1997.

Magazines

Boucher, Jim "Sneak a Peak at the Competition." *Bank Marketing*, March 1996: v28n3, p. 32-35.

"They Snoop to Conquer." *Business Week*, October 28, 1996: p. 172-176.

"It's Legal, It's Moral, and It Could Make You Rich." *Director*, October 1995: v49n3, p. 56-63.

Eckhouse, John "Leaving Tracks on the Net." *HomePC*, April 1997: v4n4, p. 91-98.

Eckhouse, John "How to Find Anything on the Net." *HomePC,* June 1996: p. 88-96.

Hise, Phaedra "Getting Smart On-Line." *Inc.*, January 1996: v18n4, p. 59-65.

Maloff, Joel "Do Execs Get the Net?" *Internet World*, November 1996: v7n11 p. 64-68.

Vine, David "I, Spy." *Internet World*, March 1997: v8n3, p. 48-51.

Stevenson, Ted and Venditto, Gus "Speed Browsing." *Internet World*, April 1997: v8n4, p. 72-90.

Dunlop, Amy "Finally, New Domain Names." *Internet World*, May 1997: v8n5, p. 16.

Jurek, Richard J. "Sharpening Your Competitive Edge." *Internet World*, May 1997: v8n5, p. 54-56.

Andrews, Whit "Planning for Push." *Internet World*, May 1997: v8n5, p. 45-52.

Vaughan-Nichols, Steven J. "Find it Faster." *Internet World*, June 1997: v8n6, p. 64-66.

Ettorre, Barbara "Managing Competitive Intelligence." *Management Review*, October 1995: v84n10, p. 15-20.

Bertnstein, Judith H. "Finding a Needle in a Digital Haystack." *NetGuide*, April 1996: v3n4, p. 79-80.

Egolf, Karen "Telcos Play the Espionage Game." *Telephony*, December 18, 1995: v229n25, p. 24.

Stuart, Anne "Click & Dagger." *Webmaster*, July/August 1996, p. 39 - 43.

Currid, Cheryl "Fight Info-Illiteracy." *Windows Magazine*, October 1996, p. 63.

Kelly, Kevin and Wolf, Gary "Kill Your Browser." *Wired*, March 1997, p. 1, 12-23.

Conclusion

After reading this book, you'll find that you probably already knew some of what was covered. After all, this isn't Rocket Science (we'll leave that to those that *should* teach Rocket Science)! You should, however, have a better idea of how to incorporate what you already knew with the new material that was introduced to create a tighter focus for your CI efforts.

Remember, it is very unlikely that you are ever going to "happen" upon a competitor's complete market plan or anything so blatant. However, with information from a few different public sources, you may well be able to formulate what it is. While not all of the information you think you need is in plain site, most of what you actually need can be found with the help of the resources listed in this book and others that you will come across in your own research. For the last time (honest!), it needs to be noted that only the practice of gathering publicly-held information—and by ethical means—is encouraged.

Just because your company is not an industry leader, that is no excuse not to be acting more like one of them! Isn't there an old saying that you need to "dress the part" that you are going after? The new president of a small manufacturing company—who had come from a background in large, corporate America—commented when he joined the smaller company that he was amazed at the lack of information they had on their competitors. Although his former competitors had been global and the new ones were literally right down the street, he knew less about the locals than he did about those half-way around the world! The practice of Competitive Intelligence is a serious matter and should be an integral part of any business owner's long range plans. That does not mean that a business has to employ a whole department to pursue this— having even one person responsible for CI would be a good start. And there is always the option of hiring an outside agency to handle the CI efforts for a business. Or, it may be possible to add CI to an existing employee's duties (yours maybe?), so long as it does not interfere with other responsibilities—that may in turn jeopardize the CI efforts.

Once you have the systems in place and the resources narrowed down, you'll probably find that the time involved is not that great. You can scan the news regularly for anything that may come along and rely on the resources you have researched and organized for specific informational needs. Should there be a particular news item that affects your industry, you can check with your industry experts; maybe zero in on the trade publications and associations to see if anything is hitting there yet; maybe check out the news groups or mailing lists for the current buzz.

As has been said before, if you don't think your competitors are doing this—think again! As the marketplace becomes more globalized, those markets are getting more competitive. To survive today and prosper into tomorrow, you really have no choice. A well-researched plan that includes strategy based on your CI efforts will carry you through that tomorrow. Don't make this one of those situations where you will say to yourself, "If only I had seen this coming...". Don't wait to react; be proactive and look for that information and the signs to avoid the "If only..." and become the "I knew that!"

Index

U

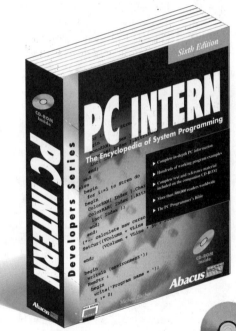

Nets and Intranets With Win95
Getting Connected

Windows 95 has a surprisingly rich set of networking capabilities. Built-in networking delivers an affordable and easy way to connect with others and benefit by sharing resources—files, printers, and peripherals. Network sharing saves you and your organization time and money and adds convenience.

Another great benefit of Windows 95 Networking is its ability to let you run an Intranet. This book and companion CD-ROM has all the pieces that you'll need to set up your own internal World Wide Web server (Intranet) without the expense of using an outside Internet Service Provider.

**CD-ROM
Included**

- A practical hands-on guide for setting up a small network or Intranet using Win95 or Windows for Workgroups 3.11.

- Take advantage of Windows 95's built in options so you can immediately use its networking features—

  - Shared printers
  - Easy-to-use groupware
  - E-mail and faxes
  - Additional hard drive capacity
  - Centralized backups
  - TCP/IP

- Step-by-step guide to getting and staying connected whether you're in a small office, part of a workgroup, or connecting from home.

- Perfect for the company wanting to get connected and share information with employees inexpensively

Author: H.D. Radke
Item #: B311
ISBN: 1-55755-31-4
SRP: $39.95 US/54.95 CAN
        with CD-ROM